COMMUNICATIVE LANGUAGE TEACHING IN PRACTICE

Communicative language teaching in practice

by

Rosamond Mitchell

CiLT

Centre for Information on Language Teaching and Research

First published 1988
Copyright © Centre for Information on Language Teaching and
Research
ISBN 0 948003 87 1

Printed in Great Britain by Warwick Printing Co. Ltd.

Published by Centre for Information on Language Teaching and
Research, Regent's College, Inner Circle, Regent's Park, London
NW1 4NS

CONTENTS

FOREWORD

Since 1976 the Scottish Education Department has funded a series of research projects at Stirling University concerned with various aspects of the teaching and assessment of foreign languages in Scottish secondary schools. This research has informed and supported the changes in curriculum and assessment which have been taking place in recent years. The programme of research began in October 1976 with a project on 'Skills and Strategies of Modern Language Teaching' which was associated with the *Tour de France* curriculum development project set up by the consultative Committee on the Curriculum. The first project overlapped with the formal and summative evaluation of *Tour de France* which in turn overlapped with the Communicative Interaction Project. Research has recently been conducted also into the school-based assessment of communicative foreign language skills in the middle years of secondary schools. Between March 1983 and May 1984 the team also conducted an examination of the potentialities and limitations of the microcomputer in the teaching of foreign languages.*

The Communicative Interaction Research Project was concluded in September 1983. As a series of snapshots of a minute and continuing sample of classroom practice and of teacher development within that process, the report is a valuable document and illustrates a good pattern for 'action research'. During the life of the project the process of the research itself was influential in furthering the development of the use of the foreign language in communicative contexts, since the researchers' continuing observations were used as a basis for discussion in many meetings of teachers and in-service training occasions. As a result the situation to be found in many classrooms today has moved on from that outlined in the research report, and we now find significantly more use of the foreign language in a more widespread awareness of the

---

Microcomputers and foreign-language learning in secondary schools. R Johnstone, I MacLean. University of Stirling 1985.

nature of communicative interaction. The research could therefore be said to have stimulated action. Teachers accepted the validity of the research because it operated in their own recognisable reality, and so communicative interaction took place, not only in the classroom, but between researchers and teachers. This interaction has played a pivotal role in our curriculum development, culminating recently in the commissioning and issuing to all secondary schools of a *Handbook of communicative methodology* (R Johnstone, University of Stirling 1987)* which takes forward the work so fruitfully begun with this present project report.

A Giovanazzi
HM Inspector of Schools

November 1987

---

*To be published by CILT early 1989.

PREFACE

This book is based on the final report of a research project on foreign language teaching carried out in Scottish secondary schools between 1980 and 1984. The project was funded by the Scottish Education Department, in the Department of Education at the University of Stirling; its full title was *Communicative Interaction in Elementary Foreign Language Teaching in Formal School Settings*. The C1 Project was co-directed by Richard Johnstone, Senior Lecturer in the Department of Education, and by the present author, who was also employed as its sole full time research worker.

In the late 1970s and early 1980s, substantial changes were taking place in foreign language teaching in Scotland as elsewhere. Partly motivated by imminent changes in the curriculum associated with the publication of the Munn and Dunning Reports and with the introduction of the new Standard Grade examination, but mainly inspired by a felt need to find a new rationale and new methods for their work in teaching foreign languages to all pupils in the early years of secondary schooling, many Scottish teachers were turning to the new ideas of 'communicative' language teaching. Through the mechanism of the CI Project, the present author had an exceptional viewpoint from which to witness their attempts to turn these new ideas into effective classroom practice.

This book provides a record of these attempts. Given the general scarcity of research-based accounts of the foreign language classroom in British schools, it is probably a unique record, which it is hoped will be of continuing interest to all concerned with the further development of language teaching methodology, as well as to those with more general interests in the mechanisms of innovation and curriculum change.

My personal thanks must be expressed here to the many people who made possible the original research project, as well as to those who assisted with the production of this book. Firstly, the role of the Scottish Education Department must be recognised, in funding at the University of Stirling over a ten-year period the series of research projects concerned with aspects of foreign language teaching of which the CI Project was one. This level of support regrettably remains highly exceptional in British education, where research into the business of teaching and learning languages other than English remains relatively neglected and under-resourced.

The second group who made the whole enterprise possible were the schools, teachers and pupils who cooperated so generously in the different phases of the Project. Within this group, very special thanks are due to the teachers who participated in the action research phase, which involved them in considerable extra work, as well as in sometimes painful processes of self-evaluation. Their commitment to the improvement of foreign language teaching, and their willingness to try new approaches and to reflect constructively on failure as well as on success, are apparent throughout many pages of this book.

I must also thank the many colleagues at Stirling University who provided advice and support throughout the research work reported here. Among these, particular mention must be made of Richard Johnstone, whose creative thinking about foreign language teaching was a constant stimulus throughout the period of our research collaboration at Stirling. (The other main publication arising from the CI Project, the 'Handbook on communicative methodology', also being published by CILT, is authored by him.)

My thanks are also due to John Trim and to the staff at CILT for their editorial advice in the revision of the original manuscript. And lastly, I am grateful to my husband Christopher Brumfit for his encouragement and support in the completion of the enterprise.

Rosamond Mitchell
Centre for Language in Education
Department of Education
University of Southampton

July 1988

INTRODUCTION

Since the mid 1970s, the international interest in developing a 'communicative approach' to L2 teaching, first popularised in the context of the teaching of English as a foreign language has been manifesting itself in relation to FL teaching in British secondary schools.

'The communicative approach' is an umbrella term, covering a wide-ranging set of developments in L2 teaching, concerning the inputs to L2 learning, its goals, its processes and its outcomes. This movement has been influenced significantly by recent theoretical developments in sociolinguistics and psycholinguistics. Most strikingly, from sociolinguistics, the 'communicative' movement has taken the notion of 'communicative competence', as the basis of an enlarged view of what it means to know a language, and therefore as the basis for a reformulation of the goals of L2 teaching. From psycholinguistics have come the notions that learning a foreign language has much in common with processes of acquiring the first language, and that active involvement in using the target language to achieve real communicative ends makes an important contribution to developing proficiency in the language itself. (See Appendix 1 for details.)

These new ideas became available to FL teachers in Britain at a time when they were likely to be receptive. The comprehensivisation of the British school system, and the consequent extension of FL instruction to virtually the whole school population in the early years of secondary schooling, precipitated a crisis of confidence within the FL teaching profession. The traditional objectives and methods of FL teaching in British schools appeared unsuited to the new situation; many pupils were being alienated from the process of FL learning and dropping out as soon as they could, having failed to learn anything very much of the target language offered to them (usually French). The quest for a new approach for FL teaching in the special circumstances of British schools (i.e. the schools of a society without strong instrumental motivation for FL learning) therefore began.

From the mid 1970s, a range of curriculum development initiatives have attempted to reformulate the objectives, syllabus, methods and assessment techniques of FL teaching in schools, at least in the elementary stages. In Scotland, the 'communicative' approach to FL teaching was pursued most vigorously initially in the first two years of secondary schooling (S1/S2), the 'common course' stage. This could be seen most obviously in three significant curriculum development initiatives of the later 1970s, one, the *Tour de France* Project nationally-organised and two, the Strathclyde *Eclair* initiative and the Lothian Graded Levels of Achievement in Modern Languages (GLAFLL) Project, at local authority level. It is these projects which form the context for the research study reported here. (See Appendix 1 for details.)

But what does the 'communicative approach', as interpreted in the British classroom, amount to? There have been other concerns underlying the wave of development in British FL teaching, in addition to the theoretical insights deriving from socio- and psycholinguistics - influential though these have been. Firstly, in all these initiatives a prime concern has been to develop a FL curriculum which will actively involve the learner, hopefully using both intrinsic motivation (by making courses more 'relevant' to the presumed needs and interests of school age learners), and extrinsic motivation (e.g. through the award of stage test certificates).

Secondly, some current non-language-specific developments in educational theory have played a part, most notably contemporary moves towards the more precise specification of educational objectives in behavioural terms (and a corresponding interest in criterion-referencing as far as assessment is concerned).

While current FL curriculum development initiatives have their own individual character, and may place different emphasis on different aspects of the teaching-learning process, nonetheless they broadly share a commitment to a general set of principles, which can overall be characterised conveniently as the 'communicative approach'. These principles include:

1. The equation of FL proficiency with FL communicative competence.

2. The analysis of learners' FL 'needs', and a more explicit specification of language learning objectives in behavioural terms.

3. At least partial organisation of the target language syllabus in notional-functional terms.

4. Some commitment to individualisation of the syllabus, to the democratisation of the teacher-pupil relationship, and to 'learner autonomy'.

5. Use of cooperative learning activities such as games, simulations and role play, and the use of non-whole class organisational patterns (e.g. group and pair work).

6. A commitment to using the target language as a medium of classroom communication.

This report is concerned with a particular dimension of the 'communicative approach' as it operates in British (more particularly, Scottish) schools: with its methodology. What is the pattern of teaching obtaining in classrooms where the development of learners' communicative competence is a conscious goal, and where the teachers believe themselves to be operating more or less in accordance with the 'communicative' principles listed above? More particularly, what opportunities are being provided in these classrooms for learners to experience the communicative, message-oriented use of the target language, which as we have seen is judged critical by many theorists for effective second language acquisition?

Constraints on communicative FL experience

However explicit the commitment to developing the learner's communicative competence may be, the provision of extended experience of message-oriented FL use for him or her is problematic in a British context. Most British adolescents have no routine contact with speech communities using the most commonly taught languages; many have never even met a native speaker of French or German. While many schools put considerable effort into prompting exchange visits, penfriend schemes, etc, such contacts are only intermittent and cannot be relied on to provide the majority of pupils with any substantial language contact. If pupils are to gain substantial experience of target language use for communicative purposes, therefore, it must be within the classroom framework; and the only fluent speaker of the target language with whom they are likely to be in regular contact is their own class teacher.

Special obstacles seem to lie in the path of communicative FL use in the British classroom however. The ratio of fluent speakers to learners is that of one to many; more importantly, teacher and pupils typically share English as their first language (and even where they do not, all are likely to be fluent English speakers). Thus - unlike the situation in many EFL classrooms, where the target language is often the only available means of communication between teacher and pupils - the target language is an optional means of communication, constantly in competition with the shared native language. The ever present availability of an efficient means of fulfilling the many immediate communicative needs involved in managing the language classroom is a powerful factor militating against adoption of the target language, so relatively inefficient for these short term purposes, as the communicative norm.

To propose to British FL teachers that they should systematically develop the use of the target language as a substantive means of communication with their pupils is not unproblematic therefore; previous methodological initiatives in a similar direction (most notably the 'direct method' school) are known to have had only a marginal impact. The general motivation for the research study reported in this book was therefore to discover the extent to which even a typically 'committed' group of teachers found it possible to use one target language (French) with their beginners' classes.

Practice and communicative FL use

In studying this issue, it was first of all necessary to distinguish primarily 'communicative' uses of the target language from practice uses. (It was assumed that the L1 was always used for message-oriented, communicative purposes.) The following definition of 'communicative' FL use was therefore developed:

> *Any instance of FL use, productive or receptive, will be considered 'communicative' if it appears that the people involved in producing/attending to the discourse have another purpose/intention additional to the general purpose of modelling/practising/displaying competence in formal aspects of the target FL.*

This definition recognises that almost any conceivable use of the target language in the British classroom, between teachers and pupils who share a common (usually, native) language already, will have an inescapable general practice function, of familiarising the pupils with the forms of the foreign language. (If the participants merely wish to communicate effectively with one another, they would do so in English.) It restricts the term 'communicate' to that subset of FL utterances for which some additional purpose can be detected. The definition is neutral as to the nature of that purpose, which may be informational, instrumental, phatic, etc; it is also neutral as to the linguistic channel being used (communicative FL use may involve any or all of listening, speaking, reading, writing), and as to the length of any instance of FL use which may be considered 'communicative'. One-word utterances may be considered to be instances of communicative FL use, as may entire teaching episodes.

The operationalisation of such a definition gives rise to problems, given its dependence on the interpretation of the subjective intentions of participants, which can never be directly accessible to an observer. When the teacher says *bonjour*, is she greeting the class, or modelling how to greet? Contextual information, linguistic and non linguistic, may provide more or less convincing evidence regarding the nature of the participants' intentions. Clues such as the predictability or otherwise of utterances, the 'newness' of information conveyed, the types of responses expected and accepted, and the nature of teachers' evaluative comments, will often mark instances of FL use as primarily 'practice' or 'communicative' in purpose, and demonstrate the existence of a consensus regarding their purpose between speakers and hearers, teacher and pupils (Littlewood, 1977; Mitchell and Johnstone, 1981; Morrow, 1981). Indeed, the 'rules' for what constitutes appropriate interaction at particular moments are made more explicit in classroom discourse than in almost any other kind of talk (Sinclair and Brazil, 1982). In general, teachers normally make their expectations for any given teaching episode sufficiently clear for an observer to decide whether or not they intend it to have a communicative dimension. The analysis in this report is thus generally based on an observer's interpretation of the teacher's moment to moment intentions for the type of language experience being fostered among his/her pupils.

The Communicative Interaction project

The Communicative Interaction Research project, based at Stirling University and funded by the Scottish Education Department, ran from October 1980 to September 1983. The project started from two major assumptions: a) that 'communicative competence' was a desirable objective for FL secondary schools, and b) that classroom experience of communicative FL use might be expected to contribute to pupils' acquisition of communicative skills. Accepting these starting premises, the project set itself a limited overall purpose: to investigate how far it was possible to provide such 'communicative FL' experience for 12 and 13-year-old beginners, within the formal context of the secondary school classroom; what conditions seemed necessary for extensive CFL use to be feasible in this setting; and what problems, 'costs' and constraints might be encountered.

Location of teacher sample

In order to investigate these issues, it was first of all necessary to locate a group of teachers committed to the 'communicative approach' to FL teaching, in whose classrooms empirical studies could be carried out. This was done through the networks of the three Scottish curriculum development initiatives at the S1/S2 level, described earlier as sharing a common commitment to the development of pupils' communicative FL competence. Richard Johnstone, co-director of the Communicative Interaction Project, was also convener of the SCCML Working Party responsible for the *Tour de France* project; the promoters of the GLAFLL Project and the Strathclyde *Eclair* initiative also agreed to the involvement of some of **their** teachers. While the numbers of teachers involved in different phases of the Communicative Interaction Project varied, all had in common some prior degree of commitment to innovation, and were engaged in the development and/or implementation of some or all of innovative objectives, syllabuses, teaching strategies and assessment procedures, directed towards the development of pupils' communicative FL competence.

Overview of empirical work

The interview survey

The work of the research project was divided into several stages. Firstly, a sample of 59 teachers of modern languages in twenty schools with experience of at least one of the three developmental projects was selected, and these teachers were interviewed in depth concerning their understandings of the nature of 'communicative competence', and their views about how to develop it in classroom settings. These Stage 1 interviews were conducted in 1981, and are reported in Chapter 1.

The Stage 1 interviews not only constituted an important component of the data collected for the project in their own right; they also provided the basis for the next phase of the work, involving direct observation of classroom teaching. The interview material was a rich source of ideas for further investigation in the classroom; in addition, the interviews provided an opportunity to locate schools willing to collaborate in later stages of the work.

Selection of Stage 2 schools

Four schools were invited to participate in Stage 2 being *Tour de France* pilot schools, and one each coming from GLAFLL and the *Eclair*-using group. These four secondary schools were all located in central Scotland, and all were state-supported comprehensive schools. Three were non-denominational schools, and one was Roman Catholic. Two were situated in small towns where each was the only secondary school, with a catchment area embracing stretches of the surrounding countryside. One of the remaining schools served an outer suburb of a large city; its catchment area included large local authority housing estates. The fourth school was the newest of several schools in a new town, still building up its numbers at the time of the research study.*

While teachers of several different foreign languages were interviewed for Stage 1, the work of Stage 2 was (after a trial period) limited to French, by far the most commonly taught language in Scottish secondary schools. Altogether, fourteen teachers of French were involved in Stage 2, in 1981-82; during this period two visits, each lasting a fortnight, were paid to each of the participating departments. A schedule of these visits will be found in Appendix 3.

Stage 3 of the project, a longitudinal case study of a single teachers' work with a new S1 class, is reported elsewhere: Mitchell and Johnstone, 1986

*To preserve anonymity the names of the schools have been changed in this report.

CHAPTER 1

TEACHERS' INTERPRETATIONS OF THE COMMUNICATIVE APPROACH

INTRODUCTION

The first phase of the Communicative Interaction Project consisted, as indicated in the introduction, in a survey of the views of teachers currently engaged in innovation, regarding what constituted 'the communicative approach' to FL teaching.

An approach was made to those responsible for promoting the three major Scottish curriculum development initiatives which were known to share a commitment to the development of pupils' communicative FL competence at S1/S2 level. The project leaders' aid was enlisted in identifying the sample of 'innovating' teachers required for the survey. The aim was to identify approximately 60 such teachers. It was assumed that they were most likely to be found not as scattered individuals, but clustered in 'innovative' departments; the plan therefore was to locate about twenty such departments and ask for volunteers for interview from within them. One-third of the sample was to be drawn from the group of schools associated with each of the three 'communicative' curriculum development initiatives.

The identification procedure varied somewhat between the different initiatives. In the case of the *Tour de France* Project, it was assumed that the 'pilot' departments were all 'innovative' in character, and seven schools were selected at random from the pilot schools in Central Scotland. For the other two projects, the project leaders were in each case invited to nominate about twelve schools which they felt were strongly involved in their curriculum initiative, and two groups of seven schools were selected at random from these lists. Twenty of the 22 schools approached responded positively and between them produced 59 volunteer teachers for interview.

These Stage 1 teacher interviews were conducted during the summer and autumn of 1981. Seven *Tour de France* pilot schools were visited, seven Lothian GLAFLL schools, and six Strathclyde

Eclair schools. The number of teachers interviewed per school ranged from one (in one school) to five (in two schools); the average number per school was three. In all, the *Tour de France* schools produced 22 volunteers for interview, the GLAFLL schools 21, and the *Eclair* schools sixteen.

However, teachers could not be allocated as clearly to individual curricular initiatives as these figures suggest. It turned out that several schools among the *Tour de France* group were also using *Eclair* with certain classes; four of the GLAFLL schools were using *Eclair* with French classes, and one was using *Tour de France*.

A few individuals who had recently changed schools had personal experience of more than one of the three initiatives; a couple of people also volunteered to be interviewed who were not involved in the major initiative with which their department was identified (e.g. an Assistant Head Teacher in a *Tour de France* pilot school, and a Principal Teacher in another, who had *Eclair* experience but had themselves so far taught no *Tour de France* classes). In interview, these teachers were encouraged to draw on all relevant experience.

Of the 59 teachers interviewed in total, 36 claimed experience with *Eclair*, 26 with *Tour de France*, and twenty with GLAFLL. Ten teachers claimed combined *Eclair*/GLAFLL experience, eight combined *Eclair*/*Tour de France* experience, while five claimed *Tour de France*/GLAFLL experience. Teachers' other current involvements with S1/S2 French, in both cases as a short term measure until the *Tour de France* course became generally available; six GLAFLL teachers drew on their experience of using two other commercially produced courses in S1/S2 (the French course *Tricolore*, and the German *Vorwärts*).

In almost all the schools visited, promoted staff figured strongly among those presenting themselves for interview. In all, 21 Principal Teachers (whether of 'modern languages' or of French or German) were interviewed, as well as two Assistant Head Teachers and several Assistant Principal Teachers. Their reported length of involvement with the various curricular initiatives varied from four years to an initiation in the current session. Three Lothian Principal Teachers claimed involvement with GLAFLL from the very beginning; a similar number of Strathclyde *Eclair* schools claimed 'pioneer' status. But only in one or two schools was there any apparent feeling that the phase of innovation was over, and that things had settled into a new routine. Even on the materials front, the imminent commercial availability of *Tour de France* meant that several 'innovative' schools were in a phase of transition to that course, whether from 'home-made' materials or even from *Eclair*.

To provide a preliminary indication of individual teachers' commitment to the process of innovation, the interviewer began by asking them some questions about their general involvement in development activity. However, of those who said they had not been involved in this decision, no less than eighteen explained that they had arrived in their present post subsequent to the departmental decision to innovate having been made. This left only five teachers in the sample who said they had been on the spot, but without being involved in making the decision.

Answers to a question about sources of information concerning the various innovations underlined the importance of inservice training and the regional advisory services, which between them were mentioned by a substantial majority of teachers. (The nationally organised inservice meetings organised for pilot teachers were mentioned most frequently by the *Tour de France* users while local advisers figured prominently as sources of information for *Eclair* and GLAFLL.) Contacts with other teachers were also an important source of information; promoted staff were explicitly mentioned by nine unpromoted teachers, and other 'grapevine' contacts by a similar number. Written documentation was mentioned as a source of information by seven people, while training colleges were mentioned by three newly-trained probationers.

While inservice training was a prime source of initial information for many teachers, only a minority (26) claimed any sort of ongoing involvement in inservice activity (whether in a working party or simply by attending meetings, etc) relevant to the innovation, external to the school itself. This minority included a small group of 'activists', mostly promoted staff who had appeared publicly as promoters/demonstrators of particular innovations, either by giving talks at inservice meetings, or by allowing their teaching to be observed and in some cases videorecorded for public showing. This group of ten teachers turned out, not surprisingly, to be among the most articulate of the interviewees.

In summary then, the strategy used to locate the group of teachers interviewed for this Stage 1 survey seems to have been reasonably successful. It was clearly not a random sample of Scottish FL teachers; everyone interviewed was indeed engaged in some way in the process of innovation, if only in the sense of getting used to a new language syllabus, coursebook and/or assessment strategy. However, the true 'activists' were a minority even within this sample, outnumbered by those who can perhaps best be described as 'secondary innovators': those who found themselves committed to innovation perhaps because of departmental policy, initiated by an 'activist' principal teacher, and who were facing the task with varying levels of enthusiasm. In between was another group, who while not activists in the public sense of speaking at meetings, getting involved in working parties etc, were initiators of innovation on their own home ground. Thus a fairly wide range in degrees of commitment to innovation existed within the group as a whole, leading to an expectation that a fairly wide range of views regarding the theory and practice of communicative FL teaching would be expressed.

ANALYSIS OF INTERVIEWS

With the teachers' permission, all interviews were audiorecorded, and the recordings were subsequently transcribed. The analysis of the interview material has been based on these transcripts. A set of fifteen themes was derived from the original interview schedule, taking into account the extent and character of actual teacher comment in response to the original questions (which led in some cases to the sub-division, in others to the fusion, of the original schedule of topics). These themes were as follows:

For each theme, a category system for the analysis of teacher comments was developed from inspection of a sample of twelve transcripts. All teacher comments judged to relate to each theme were categorised accordingly, and a set of tables was produced showing the number and type of comments made for each theme. (These tables have not been reproduced here.) On the basis of these tables, a narrative section has been written for each theme, giving an account of the types of comment made together with some quantitative indications regarding the representativeness of the different comment types. These sections, illustrated with a limited selection of direct quotations taken from the actual transcripts, form the main part of this chapter.

1. Teachers' reasons for involvement in innovation.

2. Aspects of curriculum projects perceived as *new* by teachers.

3. Teachers' understandings of 'communicative competence'.

4. The appropriacy of 'communicative competence' as an objective for schools FL teaching.

5. The relationship of 'communicative competence' with other objectives of FL teaching.

6. The choice of syllabus for the 'communicative approach'.

7. Methodology (general principles).

8. Running role play activities.

9. The use of FL and L1 in classroom management.

10. Reacting to error.

11. The place of 'grammar explanations'.

12. The place of writing.

13. Paired and group organisation.

14. Teacher-pupil relations and teacher skills.

15. Problems and constraints.

Theme 1:   Teachers' reasons for involvement in innovation

The teachers were all asked to explain the reasons, as they understood them, for their department's having become involved in innovation. While over a third made it clear that the initiative had come from someone else (adviser or head of department), the vast majority also made it clear that they had personal sympathies with the change and were able to advance substantive reasons for it.

Firstly, there was an overwhelming expression of teacher dissatisfaction with existing courses and syllabuses for S1/S2 common course language teaching. Pupils (and even some teachers!) were bored; cumulative courses organised round the abstract study of grammar were inappropriate in their goals for some if not all pupils, and were simply too difficult for many, who consequently became unmotivated, made trouble, and/or dropped out:

> We were all very dissatisfied with the course that we were using (...) and what we were achieving in teaching the children French. I think many of us used to have sleepless nights trying to justify what we were doing, talking about three cats sitting on a wall. What use is that when they leave here? (...) And also, the course that we were using meant that some of us were screaming to have the classes set round about Christmas (...) because it was such a cumulative type of course that we were using, and many people were totally lost in the class. (Teacher 29)

> It was very difficult to hold the interest and involvement of the bottom sections with the type of work we were doing. (T24)

> In the top set even it was a fairly abstract exercise (...) and it became an awful slog. And from then on right the way through to the exams, the only thing that they had in front of them was the exam. (...) The high dropout rate was really worrying us. (T59)

The teachers' positive reasons for turning to the innovative projects were in many respects simply mirror images of these dissatisfactions. It seemed to many that the new projects offered learning goals more appropriate to pupils' needs and interests (more topical, more 'relevant', and/or more 'useful'), and that standards were more realistic, with at least some stated objectives being attainable by all pupils. The new projects were thus seen as potentially more interesting and motivating for pupils; the possibility of certification at elementary levels was mentioned as a specific motivating factor by several of the GLAFLL group. Individual teachers added a scatter of other reasons for involvement: one *Tour de France* recruit mentioned the 'Scottish' character of the project, another its use of 'mastery learning' ideas: one GLAFLL supporter said the assessment scheme fitted his school's commitment to criterion referencing, another said the project allowed opportunities for contacts with other teachers, and a third that it met a need for greater accountability to parents and pupils concerning the nature of learning objectives. But the following quotations represent many more teachers than the individuals who articulated them:

OBJECTIVES APPROPRIATE

> *We now actually feel we are teaching useful things to the junior pupils. That is, if they drop French or German even after one year, or after two years, which they can do in this school, then we feel that they have got this core of knowledge which will actually serve them well if they ever go abroad. And the children are actually quite keen to use it. We have found that the response in class has been quite good. They are on the whole much more willing to participate in class than we perhaps, as teachers, ever thought they would do.* (T58)

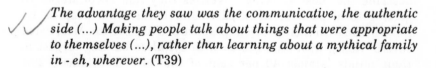

> *The advantage they saw was the communicative, the authentic side (...) Making people talk about things that were appropriate to themselves (...), rather than learning about a mythical family in - eh, wherever.* (T39)

> *When we looked at the core material, we said 'Yes, these are the kind of things that children need to know'. And it is topical and colloquial. And that is why we introduced it.* (T2)

STANDARDS REALISTIC

> *Eclair could encompass a wider range of abilities and let the children see for themselves that they are achieving something, whereas before, you know, the children felt that they were under-*

achieving. They were failing to achieve the objectives that were set for them. (T55)

I think basically, GLAFLL has something to offer every child in S1 and S2. Even if they weren't going to be going on with the FL in third year, they still could achieve something at the end of the second year. I think that's really what appealed to us, that these children who had studied French or German for two years were going to get somewhere at the end of it. And that every child, theoretically, should achieve. (T46)

PROJECT MOTIVATING

The children seem far more involved in the language. They like the language a lot more, and it is just not such a boring thing any more. They really do seem to enjoy the language. (T57)

By the end of the second year, even the end of the first year, an awful lot of pupils in mixed ability classes had opted out and were becoming very bored. And I hope, and have found so far, that you just don't get that with Tour de France *to the same extent.* (T23)

> Theme 2:   Aspects perceived as *new* by teachers

At an early stage in the interviews, the teachers were asked to describe the most striking novelties they had encountered in getting to grips with their particular curriculum project, by comparison with their previous practice and experience. Most listed several items, with issues to do with **syllabus** bulking largest in their minds (almost 40 per cent of the total mentioned). The syllabuses of the new projects were generally described as de-emphasising the systematic study of grammar, as functionally organised, and as concentrating on 'relevant', behavioural and/or communicative objectives. Many said the balance of emphasis between the 'four skills' had shifted, away from writing in particular, and in favour of speaking. Smaller numbers mentioned the 'personalised' character of the syllabuses, and commented on a perceived shift from descriptive to interactive language. Some *Eclair* users mentioned the thematic and/or modular structure of their new syllabus, and its more modest scope. A few *Eclair* and

Tour de France users mentioned the importance of unanalysed holophrases in the syllabus; a small number of the latter mentioned the appearance of 'French for classroom management'. Some GLAFLL users mentioned the change in criteria to be used in assessing pupil performance, away from formal accuracy towards communicative effectiveness.

Second in frequency to syllabus issues, teachers mentioned a wide range of materials as new for them. The *Tour de France* users were much the most likely to do so, with similar numbers mentioning the activity sheets, the English-medium 'background' materials, the explicit statements of objectives, and the grammatical explanations of the Pupil's Book. However, an even larger group referred to the *Tour de France* assessment materials as new (though only one *Tour de France* user referred explicitly to the project's 'mastery learning' strategy). Unsurprisingly, the assessment scheme was the only 'materials' item mentioned by GLAFLL users; *Eclair* users mentioned various audiovisual items (the wealth of listening materials, videos, etc). A few individuals mentioned as new for them, what might appear traditional favourites: thus flashcards were mentioned by one teacher, the existence of a coursebook by another!

Activities of various kinds were also mentioned by over half the teachers. However, most of these 'mentions' referred (favourably) to one single organisational innovation: the use of 'paired speaking', mentioned by most *Tour de France* teachers, and several *Eclair* and GLAFLL users.

The last major cluster of issues which teachers felt worth mentioning as innovative had to do with the **pupils**. They were generally described as more active and involved, and in particular as more motivated, and sustaining their interest in the subject for longer. (Several teachers here told anecdotes of pupils requesting new language items pertinent to their personal communicative needs.) A few said teacher/pupil relations were different, with the pupils becoming more autonomous and taking more responsibility for their own progress. Observed changes in overall levels of pupil achievement were, however, mentioned by only two teachers (though many said pupils could do different things from before).

Thus in response to an open invitation to talk about the innovative aspects of the various development projects, the teachers raised several important themes which were to recur in later discussion. However, it is striking that at this stage in the interview they chose in the main to talk about matters **other** than the methodology of communicative language teaching. They were of course questioned directly about this later in the interview, and then had much to say about it, as later sections will show. But among the many novelties of the various projects, methodology was by no means the most salient for teachers, at least on the evidence of their answers to this question.

Theme 3:   Understandings of 'communicative competence'

After describing their particular contacts and involvement with the various developmental projects, the teachers were asked a more general question: to outline their understanding of the concept of 'communicative competence' in a foreign language, as a target for FL teaching in schools. As a follow-up, prompting question almost half the teachers were also asked to define 'success', in terms of the FL communicative competence which might be expected of pupils completing the S1/S2 common course.

Almost all teachers were able to give some kind of definition of FL communicative competence, at least after the 'prompting' question; only two teachers declared themselves stumped by the request, although a few more replied by describing communicative **processes** rather than outcomes. There was an overwhelming consensus that the core element in 'communicative competence' was the ability to join in oral, face-to-face interaction: *understanding what is said to you, and being able to make yourself understood,* as many teachers put it. Only a few teachers defined it as involving productive, 'speaking' ability alone, and even fewer as involving 'understanding' alone. However, the capacity for oral interaction was qualified in a variety of ways; the definitions commonly given included restrictive references to particular interlocutors, topics, and locations, which learners might reasonably be expected to deal with. The interlocutors most commonly referred to (i.e. by a majority of the teachers) were native speakers of the target language, whether abroad (e.g. a pen-pal's family) or at home (e.g. exchange visitors); however, the teacher him/herself, and the pupil's own Scottish peers, were also mentioned as potential interlocutors. Half the teachers referred to the ability to cope with 'instrumental' topics arising from a tourist trip abroad (ordering meals, buying tickets, etc), while a slightly smaller number referred to 'personal' topics (being able to talk about oneself and one's family, expressing one's problems, etc). The school classroom was virtually the only location in which it was suggested pupils should be able to function, apart from the foreign country; the exceptions were a couple of scenarios such as *if they meet a tourist in trouble in Argyle Street*.... Skills other than listening and speaking were mentioned comparatively rarely. The ability to read signs and notices was mentioned by a minority of those who spoke about language-for-survival in the foreign country; the ability to correspond with pen pals was also mentioned as a component of communicative competence by a small number. However, a few also explicitly excluded skill in writing from their account of FL communicative competence. Of the small band who argued that communicative competence was not skill-specific, half clearly stated that its manifestation through reading and writing was the preserve of more advanced learners than S1/S2 pupils.

What did the teachers mean by pupils' *being able to understand and make themselves understood*? Apart from the qualifications just described, regarding interlocutors, topics, and language skills, the teachers typically did not analyse the concept of 'communicative competence' much further. Only one teacher (a GLAFLL founder member) included in his account reference to all three components proposed by Canale and Swain (1980) in their theoretical model of communicative competence, viz. 1. generative linguistic competence, 2. sociolinguistic competence, and 3. strategic competence. These three components were referred to individually by five, two and four teachers respectively. Additionally, seven teachers referred to a willingness or confidence in interaction (also discussed by Canale and Swain, though not included in their model). But with these exceptions, the teachers' accounts could not generally be related to an analytic model of this type.

The question of whether or not the teachers understood 'communicative competence' to encompass a generative linguistic competence is a particularly vexed one. A substantial group clearly understood the term in a very restricted sense (approximating to what Canale and Swain call the 'basic skills' interpretation). For these teachers 'communicative competence' was a limited survival competence, mainly involving the mastery of a set of unanalysed holophrases suitable to express the basic instrumental needs of tourists. It followed therefore that for this group the development of a generative linguistic competence was a stage **beyond** the acquisition of 'communicative competence', appropriate only for more able or more advanced learners.

However, for most of the teachers the concept of communicative competence was less restricted. A substantial minority did say that in 'making oneself understood', grammatical precision was not necessary. But it seemed in many cases (from examples given) that teachers were referring here to points of morphology such as gender agreement, and were not ruling out all need for mastery of syntax as a constituent element of communicative competence.

It thus seems that the teachers fell into three groups, as far as their state of understanding of the concept of communicative competence was concerned. A very small group clearly adhered to an 'expanded' view of communicative competence approximating to that of Canale and Swain: that it consists of linguistic competence plus sociolinguistic and/or strategic competence. Another group clearly held a 'restricted' view of communicative competence as a survival, phrasebook competence. But the majority could not be clearly allocated to either of these groups. While they made it clear that oral interactive competence was at the core, they were not specific about its component elements.

Theme 4:   Appropriacy of communicative competence as objective

---

Asked whether they felt the development of pupils' FL communicative competence was an appropriate objective in schools FL teaching, a large majority of the teachers unsurprisingly agreed. However, a few positively disagreed, and many more added riders and qualifications of different kinds. Several teachers said there remained a minority of pupils who failed to be interested in or motivated by the communicative objective; some had in mind a group such as the *least able in second year* (T59), while others were referring to the odd introverted individual. Most, however, seemed to take for granted the motivating power of this objective; the more commonly-expressed reservations had to do with the levels of achievement to be expected. One group felt that communicative competence was an appropriate objective, provided a range of levels of performance was accepted from different pupils. A second group felt that the 'less able' could not be expected to develop anything approaching communicative competence, under classroom conditions; a third, that the attainment of communicative competence was an insufficiently challenging goal for the 'high fliers'. (This last group partly overlapped with the group described in the previous section as adhering to the restricted, 'basic survival skills' interpretation of 'communicative competence'.)

Theme 5: Relationship with other objectives of FL teaching

Asked about the place of the development of pupils' FL communicative competence among the overall objectives of school FL teaching, a majority of the teachers said it was the main objective; a few argued it was the only, all embracing one. Fully a third, however, placed the development of pupils' communicative competence no higher than as 'one among a number' of possible objectives. Of the range of other objectives the teachers chose to mention, the achievement of passes in public examinations was most frequently referred to (with the rider from several teachers that this aim was actually in contradiction with that of developing communicative competence). The development of a conscious understanding of the linguistic system of the target FL was mentioned by over a quarter of the teachers (though several qualified this as appropriate for more advanced learners only); the development of cross-cultural knowledge and understanding was mentioned by a fifth. Smaller numbers mentioned as complementary to the development of communicative competence, the development of FL reading and writing skills (the latter again for certain pupils only, according to some). The acquisition of a generative linguistic competence was mentioned as a distinct objective by a small group, who were again equating communicative competence restrictively with basic, 'phrasebook' competence. Several more general objectives, not related to the development of language skills, were mentioned by one or two teachers only. These included the development of a generalised language awareness; learning how to learn; learning social skills of cooperation and discussion; and the acquisition of practical skills (managing classroom equipment!).

Theme 6: The choice of syllabus

Almost all the teachers were asked to comment briefly on what constituted an appropriate language syllabus, if it was one's objective to develop pupils' FL communicative competence. Almost a third made it clear that they felt the given syllabuses of *Tour de France*/GLAFLL/*Eclair* to be broadly appropriate, and some of this group elaborated no further. A slightly smaller number had some explicit criticisms to make of these given syllabuses: the *Tour de France* syllabus was criticised for lack of relevance to pupils' interests at certain points, and the *Eclair* syllabus for its situation-bound, holo-phrastic character. However, most teachers had some more general comments to make, beyond what were typically brief comments on specific syllabuses.

There was a very widespread agreement that the language material taught should be 'useful' and relevant to the learners' perceived communicative needs. Here the teachers' ideas relating to syllabus selection were obviously derived from their understanding of the nature of communicative competence, discussed above. Two-thirds of the teachers interpreted this to mean that the syllabus should cover 'personal' topics: language pertinent to personal details, family, likes and dislikes, etc. For many, language chosen to express such personal topics was the central component of the 'communicative' syllabus (though only a small minority took this argument further, to argue for truly 'personalised' syllabuses, to be negotiated with individual pupils).

A substantial group of teachers felt the syllabus should also contain the language necessary for survival in 'tourist' type situations (again reflecting a common interpretation of 'communicative competence'). However, a minority expressed clear reservations about this: for some pupils, such material was seen as too remote from personal experience, actual or potential.

No other topic area was anywhere near as salient for the teachers as these first two - personal and tourist survival language; only one further topic, that of 'classroom French', was mentioned by more than one teacher. This classroom area was referred to mainly by *Tour de France* users, but by only a few even from this group.

It was in terms of this restricted set of appropriate topics that most teachers discussed the syllabus issue. It could be inferred from the way they spoke about topics that many teachers assumed an at least partly functional organisation of the language material, but surprisingly few said so explicitly. Another small group argued that syllabuses must remain at least partly organised on structural principles: but only one teacher addressed herself to the question of the optimal relationship between functional and structural principles, if both are to play a part in syllabus organisation. Other ways of syllabus selection and organisation were referred to by a few individuals (e.g. the use of the frequency count, and of the 'situation', as organising principles); however, the whole issue was clearly less salient than that of syllabus topics in these teachers' minds.

Theme 7:   Methodology (general principles)

Next the teachers were asked to talk about those aspects of their teaching which they felt contributed most to the development of pupils' FL communicative ability. The teachers interpreted and responded to questions in this area in markedly different ways. A few took the opportunity to re-emphasise that the development of communicative competence was not their main goal; a few would not be drawn beyond saying that they followed coursebook recommendations; and there was one 'don't know'. But most had definite ideas to advance, though these varied in scope.

One said explicitly that everything she did contributed in some way to developing pupils' CFL competence! Several others seemed to share this wide view, mentioning activities (such as drills and grammar explanations) which they clearly recognised did not provide direct CFL experience but contributed over the long term, they felt, to developing communicative ability. Most teachers however were selective in answering this question, not attempting to describe their overall teaching strategy but talking about a particular group of teaching activities which they felt were making some distinctive contribution.

The activities talked about were overwhelmingly oral; only five teachers made any reference to the contribution of reading/writing activities (such as pen pal correspondence) to the development of communicative ability. Not surprisingly many teachers mentioned activities which could be related directly to the topic areas they had previously argued pupils should be able to deal with (see Theme 6). Thus three-quarters of the teachers mentioned role play and simulation activities, in which pupils were typically expected to act out some 'tourist survival' situation (asking the way, café scenes, etc); one-third mentioned some form of conversation on 'personal' topics (family, likes and dislikes, etc).

It was by no means always clear, however, that the activities talked about would have met the criteria used subsequently within the CI project to distinguish communicative FL activities from others (see Chapter 2). Of the group who mentioned role play activities, a substantial minority said that these constituted rehearsal rather than 'real communication'; from the expanded descriptions supplied by many teachers about how they organised these activities (see Theme 8 below), it would indeed seem that some did not provide significant communicative FL experience in the research project sense, but instead constituted enjoyable 'practice FL' activity.

Smaller numbers of teachers mentioned a range of activities which conformed more clearly to project definitions of communicative FL experience. These included games and competitions, interaction with FL-speaking visitors, class polls, songs, and going on trips. A few gave generic descriptions of activity types, which for example *confront children with the unpredictable* (T40), or even more generally, involve 'using the FL for real communication'. At this point in the interview, only a fifth of the teachers referred unprompted to the use of the FL for classroom management as an activity contributing significantly to the development of pupils' FL communicative competence.

The last major group of comments made in response to questions on this issue related solely to language skills and modes of involvement in discourse. Thus a large majority of the teachers said it was important for pupils to talk as much French as possible; over two-thirds spoke of the merits of paired speaking and/or group oral work. A few also said it was important for pupils to have the opportunity to take an initiating role in conversation. But amid this large body of comment in favour of oral work, substantial ambiguity remained as to whether or not communicative FL experience was intended. A small group commented explicitly that paired speaking was usually no more than drilling; the few who spoke about language laboratory work and repetition clearly had practice FL activities in mind. Conversely, the few who spoke of abandoning repetition and promoting, for example, 'gist extraction' comprehension activities, seemed to be aiming consciously at providing communicative FL experience. But for many teachers 'communicative' activities and oral, interactive activities seemed to amount to much the same thing; they apparently felt no need to distinguish different degrees of unpredictability, open-endedness, etc within the general category of oral interaction.

This lack of any strongly felt need to distinguish oral FL interaction and communicative FL use was one of the most striking features of the data at this point. Another was the bias in the activities reported (and later to become familiar from other areas of the project's work) towards the expressive and instrumental use of the FL, insofar as communicative FL experience was apparently being provided, and away from informational uses. Only a few teachers referred to FL activities which might be supposed to have any substantial 'informing' purpose (e.g. 'gist extraction' listening and reading activities, or even class polls on topics like pet ownership).

Theme 8:   Running role play activities

Just over two-thirds of the interviewees went into details about their organisation of role play activities, whether spontaneously or in response to further questioning by the interviewer. Their accounts of this key activity, advocated in some form by all three developmental projects, throw further light on teachers' understandings of 'the communicative approach'.

There were a few 'doubters': a small group of teachers who commented adversely on role play activity, saying that it did not suit their personal teaching style, embarrassed older pupils, and/or led to discipline problems. However, the vast majority who went into further details about the organisation of role play did so with enthusiasm.

The teachers clearly associated role play activities with non-whole-class forms of organisation; pair and/or group work featured at some stage in most accounts. (Some seemed not to distinguish between pupil-pupil functional drills such as are found on many *Tour de France* activity sheets and *Eclair* talk cards, involving strings of discrete two- or three-utterance exchanges, and fully-fledged role play conversations. In this discussion, however, only comments clearly relating to the latter are dealt with.)

The teachers exemplified their description of role play fairly freely. Café scenes were the most commonly-cited theme; smaller numbers mentioned various kinds of shopping scenes, mealtime conversation, finding the way, making a tourist trip, interviewing a stranger, planning an outing, choosing a present, watching a football match, camping, and running a mastermind competition.

The frequency with which teachers reported undertaking role play activity varied, but it seemed that for most it was an occasional event. Indeed a few explicitly referred to role play as strictly an end-of-unit event. There seemed to be a consensus that prior development of an appropriate language resource was necessary; not only were topics generally selected so as to allow re-use of language material already studied, but some teachers spoke of preliminary sessions in which language needs were discussed and gaps in linguistic knowledge filled.

While everyone agreed that children should have appropriate language at their disposal when embarking on a role play activity, disagreement began when teachers started to describe the procedure for the activity itself. Broadly speaking they fell into two groups: those who saw the point of role play being to give pupils an opportunity for improvisation and for creative FL use, and those who saw it as a dramatic production complete with pre-scripted 'lines' to be reproduced.

Members of both groups mentioned scene-setting in English, and the provision of 'model' conversations (taped or impromptu). But after this their account diverged. Roughly equal numbers argued explicitly that role play **must**, and could **not**, necessarily entail improvisation; a smaller, intermediate group argued that 'slot and filler' variation on a given conversational framework was all that could routinely be expected. (Those who did not see improvisation as an integral element were of course not hostile to it, and several said they would welcome it if it occurred; but they felt it could not be expected of any but the 'ablest' S1/S2 pupils.)

The teachers' accounts of their subsequent behaviour in managing the activity can be linked to these different expectations. Most strikingly, no less than fifteen teachers mentioned some degree of FL scripting, prior to acting out a given role play. This usually involved pupils writing down and memorising scripts they themselves had composed; some mentioned teacher scripting, or the use of course-book dialogue scripts. The production and use of such scripts is clearly hard to reconcile with the encouragement of improvisation - and hence the provision of communicative FL experience.

A different type of scripting was mentioned by another group, however (mainly teachers connected with GLAFLL): this involved the provision of L1 functional specifications, to guide pupils' FL conversation (often in the form of pairs of cards with complementary information in L1). Scripting of this kind clearly allows pupils some latitude in finding FL exponents to complete the task; thus it is not surprising that the group of teachers using such L1 functional scripts overlaps with the group committed to improvisation rather than with the users of FL scripts.

As we have seen, most teachers claimed to organise role play conversation (scripted or improvised) as a paired or group activity.

However, almost half said they followed up this phase with a whole class phase, in which groups or pairs presented their conversation to the rest of the class (one teacher said he had filmed the results, several audiorecorded them). This presentation phase was most popular with users of FL scripts, but was not confined to them.

On the basis of these reports, it was difficult to attach any clear single function to role play activities in 'the communicative approach'. From the perspective of the Communicative Interaction Project, it seemed that they often do not provide any significant communicative FL experience, but rather an enjoyable, confidence-building and involving form of language practice. It also appeared that in many classrooms they were not an integral part of the ongoing teaching-learning process: that many teachers saw them as an occasion for consolidating and displaying previously acquired competence, rather than developing it further. Of most concern, perhaps, were the low expectations apparently held by many teachers regarding their pupils' capacity for creative FL use.

| Theme 9: Use of FL and L1 in classroom management |

Although only a minority of the teachers spontaneously raised the issue of the 'managerial' use of the target language as an important component of 'the communicative approach', they had a great deal to say on the matter when the researcher brought it up.

Self-report data of this kind can of course yield only very limited information about the extent to which teachers have actually established the target FL as the normal means of communication in their classes: accounts of language behaviour are well known to be unreliable, given that much of the time bilingual speakers do not consciously monitor which of their languages they are using. However, the data can at least tell us about teachers' beliefs and expectations.

Arguments in favour of managing the classroom through the target language of course predate the recent 'communicative' movement in FL teaching, though they have been given a renewed impetus by it. The teachers showed awareness of this, a few mentioning a longstanding commitment to FL use, others mentioning encouragement in this direction at training college. More generally, the teachers' familiarity with the issue and relative fluency in discussing it may have reflected its relatively long standing in the ideology of language teaching.

Generally speaking, the teachers either claimed that they were using the target language 'as much as possible' (though perceptions of what **was** possible varied greatly), or said they were conscious of using the language less than was desirable. It appears that this is an issue about which methodologists have succeeded in inducing a sense of guilt in teachers, if nothing else; almost a third of this sample seemed almost to feel they were making an admission of unprofessional conduct, in 'confessing' to low levels of FL use. This large group tended to shoulder the 'blame' in a personal manner, attributing their failure to make the FL the communicative norm to their own personality, and/or relative lack of fluency in the target language, and most commonly, to 'laziness' and lack of will-power and perseverance!

Teachers outside this 'guilty' group also agreed that both personal fluency in the FL, and considerable perseverance, were indeed necessary if FL use was to be the norm, and that maintaining it could be stressful. The nature of the classes being dealt with was also seen as a governing factor by some teachers: a few argued that the norm of FL use was too much for lower sets on 'ability' grounds, a few that the general liveliness of contemporary mixed ability classes ruled it out, as 'control' would be impossible. The importance of departmental rather than individual commitment, and efforts to promote this, were mentioned, mostly by principal teachers. Several teachers said, however, that it was very difficult to establish the norm of FL use at any other time than the start of the year, with new S1 classes (some of these declared intentions of 'really making an effort' with their next intake); on the other hand, a few said establishing the norm was a slow, developmental business for pupils as well as teachers, and extensive FL use could not be expected until S2 or later.

Only a very small number of teachers suggested that the target language could or should be used exclusively (and from some members of this group such statements seemed little more than a rhetorical flourish, not clearly linked with most of their other arguments and accounts of practice). Equally small, however, was the group who clearly indicated that the only FL use in their classrooms was that necessarily incurred in presenting and practising the coursebook language syllabus. Much the larger number took the middle position that some 'mix' of the two languages was appropriate in classroom communication. Most teachers cited a range of classroom functions and activities for which they felt each language should be used. Their views are summarised in Table 1.1. While the numbers mentioning each item are very uneven, it is clear that the only area in which teachers generally felt use of the FL to be appropriate was that of organisational instructions (to do with seating, handing out/collection of materials, etc). Furthermore, several said that though FL use was feasible for organisational matters, they were not currently using it. On the other hand five areas were each mentioned by at least a fifth of the teachers as being inappropriate for FL use. This suggests that in the classrooms of many of the teachers interviewed, English was likely to be the dominant managerial language.

Table 1.1

Appropriacy of FL and L1 for classroom purposes

Proposed activity	No. teachers advocating	
	FL	L1
Informal talk with pupils	7	6
Organising instructions	30	4
Activity instructions	5	16
Explaining meanings	(not coded)	13
Explaining grammar	-	30
Teaching 'background'	-	16
Discussion of objectives etc	-	8
Correction of written work	1	1
Running tests	-	4
Disciplining	1	20

A small group of teachers did not link the use of either language with particular activities or managerial functions, but spoke in more general terms about the vital need to keep 'in touch' with their pupils. Regardless of activity, this group said, if the 'glazed look' appeared in their pupils' eyes, it was time to switch to English. This group associated the presentation of abstract ideas, and/or dense new information, with the use of English; it was also associated with any form of discussion to which pupils were expected to make a substantial contribution. Conversely, they argued that simpler, more routine interaction could and should take place through the FL, again regardless of activity or pedagogic function. Another group of teachers claimed to use regularly some form of 'language switching' (i.e. saying the same thing in both languages), again not linked to any particular activities. One teacher, however, said this had been an intermediate phase in her own development, abandoned as she gathered confidence in pupils' ability to cope with FL-only management.

Of those who commented on the complexity of their own speech (about a third of the total), a substantial majority claimed to go beyond the coursebook syllabus in their 'managerial' FL talk. Some referred nonetheless to the exercise of conscious control over the complexity of the FL talk they produced. Over a third of the teachers said they expected pupils to use at least some FL in return, and mentioned the systematic teaching of FL phrases to express routine classroom requests; a few also said they supplied other FL material on request, as unpredicted needs arose. Some teachers mentioned a degree of pupil resistance to this aspect of classroom FL use; others however commented favourably on their willingness to attempt it.

A range of arguments for and against 'managerial' use of the FL was implicit in teachers' accounts of what was appropriate, and in their descriptions of practice. But large numbers of teachers also argued explicitly both for and against an FL norm. The arguments most commonly advanced for managing things in L1 were the saving of time and gains in efficiency in running teaching/learning activities:

> *I think it makes it much easier to get the organisational things done at the start of the lesson if you are doing them in your own language. Instead of going to all the effort of quizzing a kid about six times if he is present or not. And he is sitting there not knowing what you are saying to him, you know?* (T38)

For speed of communication, you use your native language. (T35)

Less frequently mentioned arguments were a lack of confidence that pupils could keep up with extensive FL use by the teacher.

I certainly don't speak French all the time. The kids would be absolutely lost if I did that. (T15)

I do not think there is any particular value in speaking in French all the time, when some of them are not going to know what you are talking about. I prefer to be quite clear. (T8)

Linked to this view was the argument, again advanced by just a few, that extensive FL use was 'worrying' for pupils.

You see, having worked in a French school as well, where that was expected from you - I communicated in English all the time - I think the children get very worried occasionally. (T44)

The sheer 'artificiality' of ignoring one's shared native language, in favour of the struggle to communicate through one which was imperfectly known, was also mentioned by a few teachers.

On the other hand a series of general arguments was also advanced in favour of extensive FL use. Ten teachers said it brought it home to the pupils that the target language was indeed a real means of communication. A weaker version of this argument, that FL use helped to create the right 'atmosphere' in the classroom, was advanced by a smaller number. A dozen teachers suggested ways in which the norm of classroom FL use might aid the language acquisition process, as well as build pupils' confidence in the oral mode; that most commonly suggested was the development of strategies for coping with imperfectly understood material (gist extraction skills).

In conclusion, this is an issue on which the teachers' views and expectations differed widely. A few had effectively dismissed the possibility of using the FL for managerial purposes, as a timewasting intrusion into the 'real' work; a few appeared strongly committed to making it the communicative norm and were confident both that pupils could cope and that they would benefit. Most teachers, however, were scattered somewhere along a continuum between these two points, accepting that it is appropriate, and usually feasible, to use the FL at least for the simpler organisational matters, but often not doing much more than this. On the whole this seemed an area where the 'communicative' movement had yet to make a big impact on teachers' thinking.

Theme 10:   Reacting to error

Asked what a commitment to the development of learners' FL communicative competence implied for the teacher's handling of his/her pupils' mistakes in spoken language, only a couple of teachers responded with 'don't know's'. Most responded with accounts of their own practice, with or without some justificatory rationale.

A few teachers claimed that the quantity of errors produced by pupils had significantly diminished within the new teaching approach. But virtually all the teachers said they corrected errors of form in their pupils' speech at some point in their overall teaching strategy. Over a third claimed to correct routinely, whenever they noticed a mistake; the majority, however, added various qualifications and accounts of circumstances in which they would **not** correct.

Over a third of the teachers said their on-the-spot decisions about whether to correct were influenced by their perceptions of the pupil(s) who had made the mistake. This group all said they were more likely to correct an 'abler' pupil, less likely to correct a 'less able' one. The rationale advanced for this distinction had to do with motivation: it was widely held that over-vigorous correction undermined pupils' confidence and inhibited the 'less able' in particular from speaking. Only one teacher repudiated this policy of differential treatment, again on motivational grounds: it turned the less able into a laughing stock, he claimed, if they were not treated in the same way as others, and they found this disheartening.

A second factor widely mentioned as influencing teachers' decisions on correction was the nature of the errors made. Just under a quarter said they would correct any errors which impeded communication, but would not necessarily correct intelligible but defective utterances. Another, smaller group said they would ignore 'minor' errors, at least from the 'less able' child. (The most commonly cited example of 'minor errors' was that of mistakes in gender agreement.)

The third factor cited was the nature of the activity within which the errors were made. One group said they would not intervene in order to correct during open-ended conversation or other types of 'communicative' activity; a few said they would not correct errors in pupils' unprompted FL utterances in classroom management matters. However, a slightly larger, overlapping group said they **would** actively correct matters of form, where errors were made relating to a language point currently the focus of attention in the syllabus, during associated practice FL activities. (Conversely, a few said they would **not** correct errors unrelated to the current 'teaching point'.)

A fourth factor, that of class organisation, was mentioned by only two teachers. They felt all errors made in whole class interaction must be corrected, but this was not essential in paired/group work.

The teachers also had something to say about their actual correction strategies. The 'norm' appeared to be an immediate, active correction exchange, in which the pupil who had made the error was required to produce the correct form. However, a third of the teachers mentioned the use in at least some circumstances of what may be called 'echo' correction - where the teacher produces the corrected form, but does not insist the pupil does so. Another tactic mentioned particularly in relation to more open-ended activities was the use of delayed correction, with teachers monitoring performance, making mental note of errors, and conducting a brief post-mortem at the end of the activity. A few teachers mentioned more full-fledged and premeditated remedial sessions, in which common errors were made the subject of intensive practice. Some also mentioned the encouragement of peer correction.

As we have seen, one major influence on teachers' decision making in this area is their concern not to discourage pupils, particularly those seen as the 'less able'. This seems to operate for some at least as a limiting factor, deterring them from corrective measures which they would wish on other grounds to take, if they were convinced the pupils could cope.

So what is the purpose of immediate, active correction of pupils' mistakes, and insistence that they produce correct forms? Does it have a significant direct contribution to make to pupils' mastery of the FL system? One-fifth of the teachers argued explicitly that it did, at least for 'abler' pupils; only a few disagreed, or even expressed doubts on the matter. Only one teacher argued clearly that sustained exposure to the target language was sufficient for pupil competence to 'come right' in the end, and he was balanced by the couple who felt that exposure to incorrect forms produced by one's peers could have damaging effects (and hence that rigorous correction was essential).

A weaker form of the argument that 'active correction does good' was advanced by another group of teachers, who said they were concerned to develop pupils' formal accuracy as well as communicative effectiveness. This group argued that the teacher's error handling strategy was an effective means of attracting pupils' attention to the issue, and convincing them that accuracy mattered (whether or not it directly influenced their performance). This small group was, however, balanced by another who argued the opposite: that the teacher's correction strategy should be devised so as to bring home to pupils that intelligibility and 'basic message effectiveness' are what really matter, rather than formal correctness.

These arguments may only be partial answers to the question, 'why do teachers correct?'. That there may be other reasons was hinted at by a number of teachers. This group recognised, some of them self-critically, that to correct is an 'instinctive' reaction for teachers, and that it was a struggle to learn **not** to correct on every occasion. As one put it:

> *I don't want to hear something that is not very good French.* (T48)

However, whatever the reasons, there was no doubt on the evidence of these interviews that active correction was still in fashion. The argument sometimes advanced by theorists of the communicative approach, that correction has no long-term influence on the development of FL competence, had so far cut little ice in the classroom.

Theme 11: The place of 'grammar explanations'

It will be recalled that 'explaining grammar' was one of the teaching activities for which many teachers felt the use of English was appropriate. At a later point in the interview, all teachers were asked about the place of grammar explanations in a communicative approach to FL teaching.

The overall commitment of this group of teachers to talking in some form about the structure of the target language was striking. Only a very small minority said without qualification that grammar explanations had no part to play in the teaching of S1/S2 classes (because they were incomprehensible to pupils, and/or because they made no difference to the development of pupils' practical competence). However, of the large majority who saw them as making a useful contribution, many qualified their responses.

In their accounts of their own practice, some teachers claimed to discuss 'grammar' regularly and systematically, most that they did so occasionally, and a few that they did so only when pupils requested explanations. However, the examples cited by many teachers of the kind of 'grammar point' it was appropriate to discuss with S1/S2 pupils suggest that coverage of the language system actually being taught was by no means comprehensive. About a third of the teachers cited gender agreement in the article system as a point they would explain, and a similar number mentioned the presentation and explanation of verb paradigms. The only other language points cited were the case system of the noun (for German), some word order 'problems' (use of inverted forms and verb position in German), adjective agreement, the use of *est-ce que...*, the French possessive adjective and direct object pronoun systems, and the locative use of *en/a*; most of these were mentioned by only one teacher, one by more than four. This selection of examples suggests some bias towards 'trouble-shooting' explanations, which seemed more likely to be given at points in the FL system which contrast with that of English than at others.

As for the way in which they dealt with such explanations, similar numbers claimed to introduce grammatical terminology ('masculine'/ 'feminine', etc) and to avoid it. All those who commented on the issue (about a quarter of the total) said that the explanation of a particular language point should follow the familiarisation of pupils with relevant language forms, through presentation and practice, not precede it. Deductive teaching of grammar was generally condemned, and the appropriate technique was several times described as a 'drawing together' of already familiar material. One teacher said grammar explanations should be given *in short sharp bursts* (T11); only a few said they gave their pupils written grammar notes, for reference purposes. Most intriguingly, several described themselves as prefacing their grammar explanations with advice to pupils not to bother about them if they did not understand.

This last point in the teachers' accounts of practice is clearly linked to the belief, expressed by almost a quarter of the teachers, that a proportion of their pupils - for some, the majority - could not be expected to understand grammar explanations. Given this widely-shared belief, how is it that many teachers persisted nonetheless in giving them? The teachers produced a range of reasons for talking about the language system; many however commented that the reasons they advanced applied only to certain pupils. The first of two most commonly suggested reasons, each put forward by more than a third of the teachers, was that for at least some pupils, knowing the rules of a language was of practical help in developing competence in it. The second was that at least some pupils wanted such explanations, and even asked for them, whether out of sheer interest, or wanting the sense of security that 'knowing the rules' was felt to offer. A slightly smaller number said that it was helpful for pupils going on to more advanced study (i.e. to take FL 0 Grade examinations) to have been introduced to the study of grammar in S1/S2; much smaller groups said it was helpful in developing the skills of reading and/or writing, and that it made a contribution to pupils' general education (by developing 'language awareness').

By what precise mechanism does having a conscious understanding of the language system translate into better performance, as so many teachers insisted it did? One suggestion advanced (by about a fifth of the teachers) approximated to Krashen's 'monitor' theory (though this term was not used by anyone): that knowing the rules meant pupils could consciously attend to their own speech, and correct or avoid possible errors as they spoke (Krashen, 1981). The other main suggestion made was that for at least some pupils, knowing the rules somehow contributed to the development of a truly generative FL competence, helping pupils to move from 'phrasebook' knowledge to an ability to recombine the elements of the language into new and original utterances. There was, however another group of teachers who saw little merit in the provision of any grammar explanations at S1/S2 level. Ten teachers argued that such explanations were not necessary to develop FL competence, and/or that they had no detectable influence on subsequent performance. A middle position was taken by a small group who argued that while under information 'immersion' conditions, advanced language competence could be developed entirely by inductive, unconscious 'acquisition' processes, under classroom conditions systematic instruction including rule-giving was necessary. This last group

was the only one to use 'natural' acquisition processes as an explicit
reference point, in considering this issue; others may have shared
their view, but taken it for granted as too obvious to need saying.

Taken together, the sum of teachers' remarks on this subject
may be given a rather worrying interpretation. If as the evidence
suggests, substantial numbers of teachers do believe on the one
hand, that it is necessary to provide grammar explanations for
pupils to develop an advanced generative FL competence under
classroom conditions, and on the other hand, that substantial
numbers of pupils cannot benefit from such explanations, it seems
that some confusion persists in terms of the outcomes which may be
expected in S1/S2 teaching.

Lastly, just as some teachers had recognised in themselves an
instinct to correct (Theme 10), so a number of them recognised a
parallel urge to dissect and explain the language system, arising
from personal interest rather than perceived pupil needs.

Theme 12: The place of writing

A very large majority of the teachers said they introduced the
writing skill in S1/S2; only one stated explicitly that he left it until
S3. However, everyone who commented on the proportion of time
given over to writing said it was only a minor component of their
teaching strategy; many stressed the primacy of the oral skills in
S1/S2.

Teachers' accounts of the kinds of writing practice most
commonly undertaken accorded with this view of it as a secondary
skill. Nearly a third said that in the early stages writing should be
restricted to the reproduction of forms already familiar through
oral work.

Copywriting seemed to be the predominant form of writing
practice, mentioned by almost half the teachers (and many of these
said they did little else). A small range of structured writing
exercises was also mentioned by a smaller number (Q/A,
substitution, and fill-in-the blanks exercises). Only a handful of
teachers mentioned doing any sort of creative writing (pen pal
letters were the sole example); they were outnumbered by those
who said explicitly that such activities were only introduced in S3
and beyond, though a few more said they might be desirable.

Why do writing? Only a small group of teachers spoke of
writing as a communication skill directly relevant to S1/S2 pupils

(equipping them to engage in pen pal or tourist correspondence), though only one teacher explicitly rejected this view. For much larger numbers, the development of the FL writing skill was not an end in itself; they did not even try to justify this as a terminal objective of the S1/S2 common course.

Instead, two other quite different rationales for the introduction of writing received fairly widespread support. The first grouped a number of justifications for writing as an ancillary support to the processes of learning and teaching. Groups of teachers argued that the act of (copy)writing helped assimilation and retention of the language system, while the finished product provided a point of reference for revision and private study. Smaller numbers argued that writing supported the development of other individual skills (reading and speaking); copywriting in particular was seen as helping pupils learn to relate the spoken and written codes, and to spell more accurately (though several teachers professed dissatisfaction with levels of accuracy in copying). Practice in writing was also seen by a few as making a contribution to pupils' general education, e.g. by developing accuracy in copying.

As far as the teaching process was concerned, several teachers argued that writing helped to vary the pattern of classroom activities, providing 'a break' from oral work for both teachers and pupils, and even exercising a calming influence on over-excited pupils! A few mentioned its usefulness at times of differentiated work (e.g. during phases of individual oral testing, or remediation); at such times writing served as an extension activity which could be pupil-directed but virtually noise-free. One teacher suggested writing could have a diagnostic function, as inspection of pupils' written work could reveal systemic errors.

The other major rationale advanced for doing writing had to do with preparation for more advanced FL study. About a quarter of the teachers said that anyone likely to continue with FL learning needed an early introduction to the writing system, which they would eventually have to master if only to pass existing SEB examinations). Other reasons advanced by smaller numbers were that teachers, parents and especially pupils liked to do writing, or to see it done; and simply that writing was an expected component of the course they were following.

Arguments against writing in S1/S2 were very rare. However, it was clear that, as with giving 'grammar explanations', teachers wanted to distinguish among the perceived needs of different groups of pupils and had differentiated expectations for their performance in writing. As we have seen, one major justification advanced for doing writing applied only to those going on to take certificate courses; and some teachers stated positively that the writing skill was irrelevant for the 'less able'. There was some evidence of differentiated criteria being applied to written performance; in assessing some pupils' work criteria of formal accuracy were mentioned, while for others intelligibility, or even quantity, were the only criteria seen as appropriate, by a few teachers at least.

Overall, it would appear on the evidence of these interviews that writing and communication were largely unrelated concepts for these teachers. The main justifications for doing writing were presented as an aid to mastery of the linguistic system, narrowly defined, and an introduction preparatory to more advanced study. It is therefore no surprise that the writing activities described virtually all fell into the 'practice FL' domain.

Theme 13: Paired and group organisation

Teachers were asked to comment on their use of non-whole class patterns of class organisation in implementing a communicative approach, their possible advantages and feasibility.

Only a small minority of teachers said they never, or hardly ever, did group or pair work. Some expressed a preference, with more teachers favouring pairs over groups than vice versa; but a large majority claimed to be doing some form of non-whole-class work reasonably regularly. It seemed taken for granted that such sessions be given over to oral work.

A range of advantages were attributed to pair/group oral work. Over a quarter of the teachers said pair and group work promoted pupil involvement (many pointing out the quantitative increase in opportunities to speak for individual pupils). Similar numbers said pair and group work allowed pupils greater autonomy and responsibility for learning, as well as opportunities for creative FL use, and that pair/group oral work was less stressful for pupils than interaction with the teacher, allowing them to develop confidence in speaking. Somewhat smaller numbers said that pair/group work was enjoyable for pupils, and that it added variety to pupils' experience. Other advantages suggested were that pair/group work allowed for differentiated activity, including remediation, and that such work promoted cooperation among pupils. Disadvantages mentioned (in each case by small groups) included contingent discipline problems, the great organisational and managerial load placed upon teachers, and the fact that pupil errors would inevitably go uncorrected. Also, it was argued that even while actively monitoring non-whole-class oral work (and functioning as the 'galley master', as one teacher graphically put it), the teacher has to accept that a proportion of pupils will take advantage of the situation to be idle. Lastly, pair/group work was recognised (inevitably) to be noisy; however, as with the previous 'disadvantage', most teachers mentioning increased noise considered this to be a price worth paying.

Pair and/or group oral work thus seemed generally well established components of 'the communicative approach', as these teachers understood it. The extent to which such non-whole-class organisational patterns were being used to provide pupils with experience of communicative FL use as understood in this research project is of course impossible to determine at all clearly from data of this sort. However, teachers appeared to perceive little difficulty in providing the setting within which pupil-pupil communicative FL interaction might take place.

Theme 14: Teacher-pupil relations and teacher skills

The teachers were asked linked questions to do with the relationship between teacher and pupils appropriate for the 'communicative approach', and the knowledge and skills required of the teacher in order to implement such an approach successfully. One fifth of the teachers felt no significant alteration in the teacher-pupil relationship was implied by a commitment to a communicative approach. Another, smaller group argued that the 'personality' of the particular class was always the main determinant of teacher-pupil relationships, rather than the teaching approach being adopted. However, most felt the 'communicative approach' did imply some change. Over a third of the teachers felt teacher-pupil relations became closer and less formal. In illustration, a greater incidence of informal discussion was referred to, including a greater mutual exchange of personal information; most felt these developments were wholly to be welcomed. A few, however, were experiencing related tensions, for example difficulties arising from making public family circumstances (those of the teacher, as well as of some pupils). And a few commented that the teacher-pupil relationship was generally more difficult, with a deterioration in pupil attitudes and/or behaviour. A quarter of the teachers said that good discipline and control of the class were as vital as, or even more vital than, with other teaching approaches.

Several teachers commented that in order to implement a communicative approach, one must be able to cope with and to manage each item on the following list: increased levels of pupil autonomy and involvement, differentiated and/or individualised work, pair work (in which not all pupils might be speaking French), varied and unpredictable requests for FL language items which might or might not be in the teacher's personal repertoire, and increased noise level. The necessary personal qualities, again each mentioned by several teachers, were considered to be: a willingness to work harder than previously, and to interact constantly with pupils; being well organised, confident and relaxed in one's approach; personal fluency in the target FL, together with a willingness to admit one's own ignorance if necessary; a sense of humour, and an extrovert personality! Needs for a good theoretical understanding of the communicative approach, to have a selective, critical attitude to one's course-book, to work more cooperatively with other teachers, and to be flexible in one's teaching approach, were mentioned only by individuals. A range of personal qualities, and general pedagogic skills, thus predominated in these teachers' view of the necessary prerequisites for effective 'communicative' teaching. No knowledge other than personal fluency in the target language was mentioned as necessary by any substantial numbers (though a few mentioned the need to be familiar with the culture associated with the target language).

Overall, the skills and knowledge mentioned by these teachers seem generally desirable in all FL teaching, regardless of the particular approach being adopted; however, the fact that they felt it necessary to restate them, often expressed as aspirations for the profession rather than realities, does suggest some continuing unpreparedness among teachers for this particular round of development and innovation.

Theme 15: Problems and constraints

At the end of the interview, the teachers were asked to talk about any particular problems and constraints they were experiencing in trying to implement a 'communicative' approach. Most mentioned only one or two fresh issues at this stage. Overall, responses to the 'problems' question could be grouped around a number of sub-themes: time, resources, class size, management, assessment, teacher knowledge and skills, and pupil motivation.

TIME

Most teachers seemed to accept the time allocation given for S1/S2 FL teaching as adequate for the communicative approach as they understood it. A small group commented that they would like more teaching time, and/or to have their time differently arranged (e.g. fewer double periods). Another group, mostly GLAFLL teachers, said finding time for assessment was a problem; finding adequate preparation time was also mentioned.

RESOURCES

In contrast to the small numbers mentioning problems of time, materials-related problems were mentioned by a quarter of the teachers. These included complaints that material supplied by the various curriculum projects could be dull, hard to file and access, and/or insufficiently demanding. Some teachers also felt that there was a lack of appropriate 'authentic' materials or that the balance of skills in materials provided was wrong; a couple commented on the 'bittiness' of any functional syllabus, what they saw as related problems in the pace of pupil progress, and consequent uncertainty about standards being achieved.

'Hardware' problems were mentioned by much smaller numbers. Only a few mentioned lack of free access to audiovisual facilities as a personal problem; they were indeed outnumbered by teachers who said they personally were well off in this respect (which they saw as vital to the success of the teaching strategy). Shortage of cash for paper, cassettes, etc was mentioned as a problem by only two teachers; not having one's own classroom base, by another two.

CLASS SIZE

Only five teachers spontaneously mentioned the matter of class size as an obstacle to the implementation of a communicative FL strategy. In response to a follow-up question on this point, however, nearly a third of the teachers said some reduction in class size would facilitate a communicative approach to FL teaching, at least with some age and/or 'ability' groups. Most of these teachers claimed to be 'coping' as things were, but said more could be done with smaller groups. Several teachers argued that a communicative approach now made foreign languages into 'practical subjects', which should be taught to smaller groups as for example science subjects were.

More specifically, some mentioned the need for smaller numbers if paired and group speaking activities were to be adequately monitored, others in order to carry out demanding individualised assessment procedures. Of the smallish group of teachers who did **not** see class size as a problem, most reported themselves as already having smaller than average numbers.

MANAGEMENT

The answers to the general 'problems' question reflected yet again the teachers' concern with managerial issues. Over a quarter referred to management problems, most commonly mentioning the management of differentiation. The management of materials and of assessment were also referred to again; just two teachers mentioned difficulties in meeting school or parental demands for homework to be set.

ASSESSMENT

As we have seen, some teachers mentioned problems of time and management in relation to internal assessment. Another group mentioned the problem of a lack of 'fit' between the assessment strategy associated with their FL curriculum project, and the assessment policy of the school. Lastly, another group returned to the contradictions between the skills required, and criteria applied, in SEB certificate examinations, and the logic of the communicative approach.

TEACHER KNOWLEDGE AND SKILLS

A very small number questioned teachers' general professional readiness to tackle communicative FL teaching (some teachers' lack of personal FL fluency and/or of disciplinary control were here seen as the main problems). The need for energy and professional commitment was again emphasised by a substantial group; a few recognised that some stress was inherent in any commitment to innovation, while a demand for inservice training again emerged, from another group. Cooperation between teachers was seen as a significant issue by a small number, whether it involved team teaching, the regular sharing of a class between teachers, or finding ways of coping with teacher absence.

PUPIL MOTIVATION

Just a few teachers again mentioned matters to do with pupil motivation, in response to the 'general problems' question. A few said pupils were unresponsive to the communicative approach, e.g. due to shyness; a couple referred again to a more general lack of motivation for foreign languages. Countering these views to some extent was the single teacher who argued that increased motivation would lead to 'problems' - in coping with increased numbers wanting to do FLs in S3/S4!

CONCLUSION

The Stage 1 interviews conducted for the CI project had a double purpose: a) to survey and give an overall account of 'committed' teachers' understanding and interpretation of the communicative approach to FL teaching, and b) to identify issues to do with communicative methodology, capable of empirical investigation in later phases of the project's work.

An overview of general issues

In concluding the general account of the interview material, some major issues of concern for the further development of the communicative approach will briefly be considered.

The first of these has to do with the wide range of understandings held by teachers of the concept of 'communicative competence'. For some teachers, as we have seen, 'communicative competence' meant a restricted 'phrase book' type FL competence for survival in a limited range of tourist/instrumental situations. For others, it meant a truly generative linguistic ability (i.e. mastery of a grammatical system), **plus** sociolinguistic and strategic competence. These differing interpretations led to widely differing views as to the centrality of communicative competence among the objectives of common course FL teaching (and its appropriacy for different groups of pupils), and must surely be a potential source of confusion in any discussion about aims.

Secondly, as far as syllabus was concerned, it seemed that teachers had far more developed views to express about the choice of language skills, topics and situation than about the selection, organisation and grading of actual language material. Most teachers argued convincingly for a syllabus centring on the oral/aural skills, with a combination of personal and tourist/instrumental topics. But while they seemed to approve of the at least partly functional organisation of language material in the early units of the various development projects, they had little to say about how such a syllabus might develop at later stages. Indeed, many seemed to assume an eventual transition to a structurally-organised syllabus for more advanced learners. But how and when this transition might best be effected, was not made explicit. Indeed, the rationale for choosing one form of syllabus organisation over another at different stages was not fully developed either. It seemed that many teachers liked the functional organisation of elementary material for motivational reasons, and perhaps because it facilitated 'relevant', appropriately contextualised holophrastic learning, a form of learning which teachers felt to be accessible to most pupils. It was also clear that many felt a structurally-organised syllabus was the most effective basis for success in SEB FLs examinations. But overall it seemed that teachers have yet given little thought as to which of these two organising principles might be the more effective in developing pupils' communicative competence beyond elementary levels.

Teachers' understandings of, and beliefs about, psycholinguistic processes of language learning and acquisition are potentially of great importance in governing classroom decision-making at all levels. The comments of the teachers involved in Stage 1 suggested that most still adhered to many traditional beliefs about how language learning takes place in classrooms: for example, the provision of grammar explanations, and the correction of pupils' formal errors, were both justified by many on the ground that they make a direct and significant contribution to the pupils' internalisation of the target language system. Thus the theoretical rationale from which the 'communicative approach' derives much of its force (that the target language system is largely acquired rather than consciously learned, from message-oriented experience of its use), did not appear to have many adherents among this group of teachers. Their rationales for innovation had, it seemed, more to do with pupils' likely language needs and with motivation, than with the adoption of new theories about the language learning process.

The interview questions about grammar also cast light on a further important aspect of teachers' understanding of the classroom language learning process. Their comments on several methodological issues were qualified not only in terms of time, topic, activity, etc but also in terms of pupils' perceived differential capacity to benefit from them. Thus, as we have seen, not all pupils were expected to benefit from explanations, or from formal correction processes. While some teachers seemed to suggest that the learning strategies of individuals could vary with no particular implications for learning outcomes, most seemed to feel that for classroom learning to be effective in the development of a generative FL competence, particular learning strategies such as the application of abstract grammatical explanations were essential. If teachers believed this and also doubted some pupils' ability to apply such strategies, it is possible to account for the fact that many clearly held highly differentiated expectations about learning outcomes.

Lastly, the continuing importance of organisational matters for teachers should be remembered. These were to the fore both when talking about the biggest differences involvement in GLAFLL/*Eclair*/*Tour de France* had made in how they taught, and when discussing associated problems. The fairly general acceptance of pair work, and more limited acceptance of group work, were two of the most striking changes mentioned. However, it seems that while these organisational moves were leading to a strengthening of oral, interactive work, associated increased levels of communicative FL use could not be taken for granted; it also seemed that significant differentiation and individualisation of instruction was not being introduced by this route.

These matters of objectives, syllabus, language learning theories and organisation were not accessible to further practical investigation within the CI project, with its methodological focus. However, they are clearly crucial for the further development of 'the communicative approach' overall.

Methodological issues

These interviews could provide only limited and indirect evidence about teachers' classroom practices. However, they indicated a number of methodological issues which were to be pursued in the main empirical study. As we have seen, the teachers generally emphasised the use of oral, interactive FL activities as main components of any 'communicative' teaching strategy. Many described running such activities on a paired or group basis, with an apparent bias towards instrumental and/or expressive (rather than informational) language use. But many went further, seeming actually to equate oral, interactive FL use with communicative FL use, and making no further distinctions, e.g. between creative and structurally-controlled oral activities. This emerged particularly from teachers' comments on the use of role play activities; here there was wide variation about the degree of structuring which was felt appropriate, and the extent to which improvisation was seen as feasible. The topical and linguistic content and organisation of oral, interactive activities, whether 'real' or role play, and the degree to which they provided experience of communicative FL use for pupils, were thus confirmed as issues to be pursued in the classroom-based research.

The teachers' comments on the use of the target FL as a means of communication for classroom management matters also reinforced the view that this might be a significant issue for classroom investigation. While on theoretical grounds classroom management appears a fruitful potential source of communicative FL experience for pupils, the teachers generally held that only restricted FL use was possible for management purposes. A small number made more ambitious claims as to what was possible, but suggestions were also given concerning necessary conditions and likely constraints, which were to be the focus of later study.

CHAPTER 2

STAGE 2 OBSERVATION: ANALYSIS OF TEACHING ACTIVITIES

THE OBSERVATIONAL VISITS: PRACTICE FL, COMMUNICATIVE FL, AND ENGLISH MEDIUM ACTIVITIES

Stage 2 began in autumn 1981 with a series of non-interventionist, observational visits to the classroom of thirteen cooperating French teachers; in all, 122 S1 and S2 lessons were observed during these visits. From the notes and recordings made by the researcher present as observer throughout, these lessons were retrospectively analysed into sequences of distinct teaching activities, using an analytical framework similar to that used in a previous research study (Mitchell et al, 1981).

Briefly, the procedure was to analyse each lesson into a sequence of fairly large discourse units or 'segments', corresponding broadly to the units named 'contained segments', or 'episodes' by other researches (Gump, 1967; Sinclair and Coulthard, 1975). A segment was defined as a sizeable sequence of lesson discourse, typically bounded by framing and focusing moves (Sinclair and Coulthard, op. cit.), and within which a distinctive configuration of rules and expectations for what is to count as appropriate language behaviour is established and sustained. The individual segments into which each lesson was divided were then allocated to one of three categories, according to the apparent intentions of the teacher: 'English medium', 'practice FL' and 'communicative FL'.

English medium lesson segments were those in which the target FL appeared marginally if at all, the mother tongue instead predominating as the language of communication (the presentation of background material or of grammatical information, and the discussion of unit objectives, were common examples of such segments). Segments in which FL use predominated were divided between the other two categories. 'Practice FL' segments were those in which the forms of the target FL were rehearsed in some way, without any other substantive purpose for FL use being discernible (e.g. repetition or structure drilling). 'Communicative FL' segments were those in which some substantive purpose, additional to the purpose of rehearsal, could be detected. Individual segments were allocated to one or other of these three categories, in accordance with the observer's understanding of the teacher's intentions for the language of that segment.

Of course many segments contained individual utterances or exchanges not conforming to the intended pattern. Odd remarks in French were often made, or isolated French words or phrases were commented on, during English medium discussion, and English utterances were common, though irregular, intruders into both types of FL segment; and FL utterances or exchanges with a communicative character occasionally interrupted a structure drill or other practice FL segment. However, almost always the overall intention was sufficiently clear and sufficiently well-realised to allow for unambiguous allocation of segments to one or other category.

The next four sections of this chapter describe in turn the patterns observed in individual departments during the Stage 2 observational visits.

L1, PFL and CFL activities at Palmer High School

Palmer High School was the first of the four schools to be visited for the purposes of Stage 2. Four teachers (Teachers A - D) were observed, teaching French with the *Tour de France* course. Two were working with S1 classes and two with S2 classes. All classes were organised on mixed-ability principles.

The teaching at Palmer was generally characterised by a strong commitment to the use of French for classroom management (see Chapter 7). However, over all the lessons observed at this school at both S1 and S2 levels, by far the largest proportion of teaching segments involved various kinds of practice FL activities, rehearsing the vocabulary, structures and functions of the *Tour de France* syllabus. Considerable variety was apparent in the linguistic content and skills being practised, as well as in the materials used (flashcards, activity sheets, etc), and in organisational patterns (whole class work, group, paired and individual work). There was, however, a clear general emphasis in this practice FL activity on the rehearsal of interactive oral skills.

By comparison with the high-frequency practice FL activities, both communicative FL segments and L1-medium segments were relatively uncommon in these lessons. At S1 level, communicative FL segments were noted at a rate of fewer than one per lesson. Those that occurred could be grouped into five different types:

1. Social CFL interaction (e.g. introducing a visitor; discussing the weekend)

2. Making and doing via CFL (e.g. making sets of mini flashcards)

3. Guessing activities (e.g. 'Who am I?')

4. Role-play activities (e.g. 'Mealtime at the Garniers')

5. Games (e.g. Bingo).

At S1 level these communicative segments were always fairly brief (a couple of minutes or so), and often involved only minimal FL output from pupils (e.g. types 2 and 5 above).

At S2 level the incidence of communicative FL segments noted was somewhat greater (slightly more than one per lesson). All the types noted in S1 recurred, with the exception of Type 2 ('Making and doing'). One additional type was found which might be termed 'Creative fiction', in which pupils were asked to invent stories in FL. At this level the communicative segments lasted substantially longer than in the S1 classes (up to ten minutes or so), and there was a more consistent expectation of FL output by pupils.

Perhaps the most interesting examples of communicative activities at S2 level were the 'social interaction' segments organised by Teacher C, where pupils brought in and discussed their own holiday photos, and the 'tourist guide reports to base' role-play organised by Teacher B. These two activities afforded pupils the most extensive opportunities for open-ended FL use of any of the observed teaching segments. Lastly, at both S1 and S2 levels, the communicative FL segments almost always used the spoken word. The only exception was a guessing game involving writing, which was organised on two occasions by Teacher C. There were no communicative FL activities involving reading.

Only a few instances of substantial pedagogic activities planned to take place through L1 were observed in the course of the fortnight at Palmer High School. The first of these was a 'background' lesson at S1 level; two other individual segments involved discussion about 'what you have been learning', i.e. about language objectives. These episodes were of types not attempted in FL by any teachers. There were two examples of English-medium segments comparable to activities seen at other times being conducted via the FL; these were an episode in the only team-taught lesson observed, where English was used to verify comprehension of an FL tape-slide presentation and another listening comprehension activity. One unpremeditated L1 discussion segment occurred as the result of a chauvinistic remark by a pupil.

English medium segments were thus fairly rare in the Palmer lessons, and most of those that did occur were distinctive in character; in only two cases were L1 segments observed which resembled other, FL-medium segments in topic and activity type.

L1, PFL and CFL activities at Bloomfield High School

At the second school to be visited, Bloomfield High School, four teachers were also observed (Teachers E - H). This was again a *Tour de France* pilot school; as at Palmer, two teachers were working with S1 classes and two with S2 classes (all mixed ability). The pattern of teaching activities observed in this department was more variable, although all were generally compatible with *Tour de France*, and many deriving directly from suggestions in the *Tour de France* materials. This variation was partly due to the different stages reached by the two-year groups in their respective units of work, and partly due to different styles adopted by individual teachers.

All four teachers were observed conducting tests, but even these were of different types. The two S2 teachers each devoted several lessons to the individual administration of the *Tour de France* Theme 2 Speaking Attainment Test (pilot version), while the S1 teachers each devoted parts of two successive lessons to the administration of unit diagnostic tests ('speaking' in one case, 'listening' in the other). The S2 teachers were also observed presenting the 'background' material for a new theme (over two or three lessons).

Apart from the lesson segments grouped under these major themes of assessment and background, the overwhelming majority of teaching activities seen in S1 and S2 were directly concerned with the development of pupils' FL competence. Both teachers of S1 classes were mainly concerned with rehearsal and consolidation of the language syllabus of an early unit of work. This was achieved through a mixture of practice FL activities, and communicative activities selected so as to provide opportunities for re-use of the unit language syllabus. The latter included a variety of guessing activities (e.g. 'Who am I?'), contextualised role plays (e.g. 'Mealtime at the Garniers'; 'Meeting a stranger'), a game ('Bingo') and 'personal' discussions based on family photos. The guessing games seemed particularly successful in inducing pupils to put their FL knowledge to use to find something out. Apart from some role play activities, they were almost the only context in which S1 pupils were sufficiently motivated to 'invent' words (*Elle est Sweedesh?*), or to request new FL forms ('How do you say 'Spanish'?). The family photos were almost too interesting, sometimes stimulating L1 discussion rather than communicative FL use in group/paired settings! The role plays on the other hand often appeared somewhat stereotyped, with pupils modelling their FL utterances closely on dialogues presented in the course materials (though they did occasionally request new FL items, e.g. 'How do you say "What's your telephone number"?').

These activities which appeared to involve communicative FL use, according to the CI project criteria, were outnumbered in both sets of S1 lessons by a range of practice FL activities. The practice segments, however, had a number of features characteristic of a 'communicative' FL teaching strategy in a wider sense. Firstly, they frequently involved rehearsal of groups of functionally-related, though structurally-disparate phrases (e.g. a group of Q/A exchanges to do with people's identity, and another group of phrases to do with 'offering' / 'accepting'/ 'refusing'). Secondly, the teachers consistently attempted to contextualise and/or personalise these practice FL activities. To quote a typical example, a drill on the exchange *Qui est-ce?/C' est...* was run with live pupils as the 'stimuli' and introduced with *Moi, je suis un professeur très distrait.* 'I am very absent-minded as you know, and can't remember names!' (Teacher G).

English-medium segments were unusual in the S1 lessons. One group of such segments was related to the issue of testing; both the S1 teachers explained the purpose of diagnostic testing in L1, and it was used to discuss pass marks and criteria of correctness. Another group of L1 segments concerned the setting and checking of homework. The only extended discussion of a 'background' issue noted at S1 level was in L1 ('French mealtime customs'), as were all extended discussions of linguistic issues, a fairly common activity for one class (e.g. talk about question intonation, the *tu/vous* distinction, and the *un/une* distinction).

The pattern of activities in the Bloomfield S2 lessons was different from that seen in S1. Broadly speaking, L1 segments were more common, and communicative FL segments less so. This may, however, have been due in part to the stage the classes had reached in the course at the time of the visit.

To begin with, the S2 teachers were seen preparing for and administering the (pilot) Theme 2 Speaking Attainment Test. This test was perceived by the teachers as an achievement test of formal mastery of the language syllabus; thus preparation for and administration of the test both consisted in practice FL activity. The only communicative FL use at segmental level observed during this phase was the alternative activity provided for pupils who had done the test, a (highly unusual) instance of communicative FL reading.

Once the testing phase was over the S2 teachers moved on to the 'background' section of the next unit. They each spent at least two lessons on this material, during which the substantive language of instruction and discussion was L1. They then devoted the remaining lessons observed almost entirely to practice FL activities, presenting and rehearsing the language material of the unit most commonly via flashcard-based drills. These were 'managed' via FL to a considerable extent in one classroom, though less so in the other, thus sustaining some communicative FL use throughout these practice-oriented lessons. Additionally, ingenuity was expended to personalise and contextualise the practice activities. Thus, for example, Teacher E based several drills of 3rd person verb forms on the actions and hobbies (real or imagined) of the pupils present:

TE   *Emm, tu fais du sport?*

P1   *Oui, je joue au hockey.*

TE   *Au hockey. Et toi aussi Lynn, tu joues au hockey aussie, hein?*

P2   *Oui, je joue au hockey.*

TE   *Oui, très bien. Qu'est-ce qu'elles font alors? Qu'est- ce qu'elles font?*

P3   *Elles jouent au hockey.*

This teacher also had pupils mime various actions (washing windows, playing bagpipes, etc) as the stimulus in other drills. Interestingly, his evident concern to 'humanise' practice FL activities in various ways sometimes interfered with their intended purpose of structural drilling. Pupils trying to say something meaningful sometimes strayed away from the 'target' structure, as in the following example:

(TE has been drilling 3rd person plural verb forms, using flashcards)

TE   *Qu'est-ce qu'elles font?*

P1   *Elles marchent dans l'eau.*

TE   *Elles marchent dans l'eau. Tu marches dans l'eau, quelquefois?* ... *Pendant les vacances,* during the holidays?

P2   *Oui, elle marche dans l'eau.*

TE   *Toi, tu marches dans l'eau?*

P3   *Oui, j'aime marcher -*

TE   *J'aime marcher,* possibly, *mm mm.*

P4   *Oui, je marche dans l'eau.*

TE   *Oui, je marche dans l'eau, oui, je marche dans l'eau. Tu marches? Oui, je.... Ils marchent? Oui, ils marchent.*

In this case P3's attempted utterance seems an appropriate response to a 'real' question, interposed in the drill, but does not fit the particular structure being practised.

In these final lessons the S2 teachers also included a few all-L1 segments, for such purposes as discussing the language objectives of the new unit and giving supplementary background information. Grammar rules were rarely discussed at length in these classes, but any such discussion always took place through English.

L1, PFL and CFL activities: at Sweet Grammar School

At Sweet Grammar School the *Eclair* course was in use for S1 and S2 French teaching. All classes in S1 and S2 were mixed ability; three teachers (Teachers I, J and K) participated in the study, two teaching S2 classes, and one an S1 class. The S1 teacher was using

Unit 2 of the *Eclair* course; the S2 teachers were using Unit 6. Although all three teachers were at similar stages in their respective units of work, the pattern of teaching activities varied considerably between the two-year levels. In S1 a large majority of activities were 'practice FL' in character, providing the pupils with varied practice in the language syllabus of Unit 2. These practice FL activities included drills and Q/A exercises with a variety of pictorial stimuli (flashcards, drawing on the blackboard, etc). In addition, the teacher 'personalised' some of them, either by allowing a degree of individual choice of response in Q/A drills, or by using classroom objects as stimuli (e.g. bags, books, eyes, mouths, etc, when drilling (*ouvert/fermé*).

Activities which fully met the CI Project definition of 'communicative FL use' were much less common. Two clear examples were a 'shopping' role-play, done as a paired activity, and a 'count the claps' game.

Some activities also occurred with some claim to count as examples of communicative FL use, but not fully meeting the proposed definition. These included (a) an open ended listening activity, followed by a brief discussion (in L1) of pupils' affective reactions to the recorded text (was it funny? etc), and (b) an enactment by pupils of a 'bank robbery' scene, modelled on a pre-recorded dialogue. Even rarer, though, were L1 segments, of which only one was noted (an extended discussion of the grammatical concept of 'gender').

English-medium activities were equally rare in the S2 classes. In one class the only L1 segment was pupil-initiated (singing 'Happy Birthday' to teacher)! In the other, on one occasion a 'background' topic was introduced in L1 ('French festivals'), as was a single 'linguistic' topic (ordinal numbers), in the same lesson. Apart from an L1 recap of the content of a videoprogramme, all other S2 teaching/learning activities were FL medium at least in intention.

In both the S2 classes communicative FL activities substantially outnumbered practice FL activities. The commonest communicative FL activities were interactive, with an expectation of pupil FL output. They included a variety of guessing activities, memory games, role-play conversations, discussions about 'real life' topics and games of bingo. Each teacher also arranged a few purely receptive communicative FL experiences (such as viewing a videoprogramme, and a period of 'recreational' reading); and each on at least one occasion 'taught' pupils something they did not know, all or substantially via FL. (In one case this was a method of telling which **months have 31** days; in another, the FL assistant and the teacher together told the class about some major festivals of the French calendar.)

The two S2 teachers organised these communicative FL activities somewhat differently. One (Teacher J) favoured small group forms of class organisation and set many tasks to be carried out by pairs or threes. The other (Teacher I) ran most of her communicative FL segments as whole class activities. These contrasting organisational forms appeared to have different potential advantages and problems.

L1, PFL and CFL activities at Jespersen Academy

Two teachers of French (Teachers L and M) were involved in the Stage 2 study at Jespersen Academy. One was observed teaching a single S2 class (a 'high ability' set); the other was observed with two classes, a mixed ability S1 class and a 'low ability' set in S2. The *Tricolore* course was being used; in each case, classes were in transition between two coursebook units at the time of the visit.

The substantial Pupil's Books provided with this course figured much more prominently as an 'organiser' of instruction than did the Pupil's Books of either *Tour de France* or *Eclair* in the other Stage 2 schools. In many lessons seen at Jespersen, the entire lesson structure seemed derived directly from the Pupil's Book, with a sequence of activities being done in the order presented there. That is, while in the *Tour de France* and *Eclair* schools variation between communicative FL, practice FL, and L1 activities seemed to depend to a significant extent on teachers' personal styles and choices, in the *Tricolore* lessons the balance seemed largely determined by that proposed in the course materials.

Practice FL activities were the most common type in all three *Tricolore* classrooms. Some of these practice activities were suggested in the materials, others devised by the teachers. They included structure drills, exercises practising various Q/A exchanges, some repetition activities, reading aloud, and the taking of the vocabulary notes. *Tricolore* provides a considerable amount of material for listening and reading comprehension, which was used extensively by both teachers. Where such material (taped or printed) was presented bit-by-bit to the pupils, accompanied by detailed 'comprehension checks' but without any other goal than 'comprehension' being made explicit, the activity was considered to have a practice FL character.

While such practice FL activities were the most common of the three types in all classes, there was a clear concern on the teachers' part to link the structures and vocabulary being practised through them to pupils' personal interests and possible communicative 'needs'. This was particularly striking at S1 level, where, for example, the structures

Est-ce que tu aimes...   *Non, je n'aime pas...*

Oui, j'aime...   *je déteste....*

j'adore...

were being intensively practised. As suggested in the *Tricolore* materials, 'pets' and 'hobbies' were the chosen areas for the expression of 'likes and dislikes'. Teacher L consistently insisted (within the restricted framework of the Q/A exchange) that the pupils should 'tell the truth' about themselves and their real preferences. She became quite well-informed about pet ownership in the class and took care to ask relevant questions of individuals such as the owner of *56 oiseaux!* The exercise format was usually sufficiently open to allow pupils a limited degree of choice in what to say (if only a choice between *Oui, j'aime.../non, je n'aime pas...*).

This element of choice in 'drill' type activities appeared meaningful for the pupils (e.g. the boy who complained there had been no opportunity to express a liking for football). However, they hardly ever attempted to deviate from the 'target' structures and received little encouragement to do so. Thus one of the earliest drills of this type to be observed was introduced in the following way:

Let's see what we're going to learn to-day! Here's to-day's question: *Est-ce que tu aimes les (...)*/Here's the answer: *Oui, j'aime les ... .*

Teacher and pupils never lost sight during these drills of this overarching general purpose of mastering particular structures. The teacher's insistence on 'telling the truth', and occasional communicative FL comments and detours, while important in motivating and involving the pupils, did not affect the essentially 'practice' character of these activities.

Entire lesson segments which could be characterised as 'communicative' FL activities were uncommon at S1 level, occurring at a rate of somewhat less than one per lesson. The instances seen were of three types: information-gathering polls and surveys, games/puzzles, and 'communicative' listening and reading activities.

The last-named of these three were much less common than 'practice' listening and reading, already mentioned. But spoken or written texts were sometimes presented to pupils with much more 'open' and content-oriented instructions to guide them; in such cases the activity was considered to have a 'communicative' aspect. Several instances of texts being used in this way occurred in the S1 lessons, as when pupils listened to taped 'interviews' with instructions to find out the names of the animals being talked about, or read a story or cartoon strip with very general instructions to 'find out what happened'.

The 'opinion surveys' initiated on two occasions by Teacher L at S1 level, once concerning pets (likes and dislikes), and once concerning family membership, were the clearest instances at Jespersen of S1 pupils being required to present new and meaningful information via the FL.

At S2 level, communicative FL activities occurred with similar frequency with the 'low ability' class (also taught by Teacher L), but somewhat more often with the 'high ability' class. 'Communicative' listening and reading activities of the type just described occurred with both S2 classes, and a few games and puzzles were also seen (in Teacher M's class).

Several types of communicative FL activity were also seen at S2 level, however, which had not been observed with the S1 classes. These included 'problem-solving' tasks, and one instance each of 'extended information-giving' by pupils, of role-play, and of 'background' discussion.

'Problem-solving' tasks were in fact the most common types of communicative FL activity observed here at S2 level. Mainly following suggestions in the *Tricolore* materials, both S2 teachers ran a variety of such tasks, whose 'communicative' character resided in the fact that the stated purpose of the task was to solve a problem, and use of French was incidental to this. These tasks were frequently based on materials such as maps or timetables, and involved activities such as route-planning, or making deductions from a combination of written and visual information. (With her 'low ability' class, Teacher L carried out a map-based task first of all through English, and then a second time in French. Such segmental language switching is virtually unique in the data; the fact that the task was considered worth doing via L1 is of course evidence in favour of viewing it as a 'communicative' activity.)

English-medium segments were uncommon, at both S1 and S2 levels, in the *Tricolore* classes. Where they occurred they were to some extent distinctive in topic. Thus any substantial discussion of administrative matters took place in L1 (e.g. giving out test marks). Any 'grammar' segments (e.g. presentation of a verb paradigm) and any extended discussions of pupils' personal experiences (e.g. 'crossing the Channel') were also always L1-medium. There were also several examples of 'background' topics being dealt with in L1. Such segments were always based on some item in the *Tricolore* materials, often itself L1 medium (e.g. the weather in France; the *Tour de France* cycle race). The S2 materials also propose FL-medium treatment of some 'background' topics, however, and the teacher of the 'high ability' S2 class was seen to follow this recommendation (*comment voyager en France, les trains français*).

SUMMARY AND DISCUSSION

In summary, all thirteen teachers involved in the observational visits of Stage 2 structured their S1 or S2 French lessons from activities of the three basic linguistic types: English medium activities, practice FL activities and communicative FL activities. These three activity types occurred in varying proportions in the lessons of the different teachers. For all teachers, English medium activities were the rarest type. Communicative FL activities were commonest for two teachers only (those seen with S2 classes at Sweet Grammar School); for the rest, practice FL activities were commonest.

Adaptation in practice FL activities

However, as appears from the accounts given in preceding sections, a considerable softening of the pattern of decontextualised repetition and drill activities noted in similar data collected in 1978 (Mitchell et al, 1981) could be detected. In these CI Project classrooms, drills were typically contextualised, and topics 'personalised' even in a drill framework; structurally disparate utterances were frequently rehearsed in combination in functionally oriented drills. Thus, although practice FL activities still out-numbered other types in most classrooms, their character had altered significantly.

General character of communicative FL activities

For half the teachers in this study, activities judged to have a communicative character averaged about one per lesson; for the rest they were less frequent (though the relative frequency of the different activity types did seem to be determined to some extent by the stage of progress through given coursebook units as well as the range of activities suggested in course materials).

Only a small range of communicative FL activities occurred at all frequently in the corpus of 122 lessons. The only types of activity judged on more than three occasions overall to have a communicative character were:

- Real life/personal discussion

- Role plays and simulations

- Guessing activities

- Games and puzzles

- Problem-solving activities

- Open-ended listening

- Open-ended reading

Functional differentiation between FL and L1

If this pattern of actual communicative FL activities observed is compared with all those logically possible, certain biases are immediately apparent. Firstly, most communicative FL activities were both oral and interactive, with an expectation of pupil FL output. Recorded and/or printed texts played only a minor role, with communicative listening and reading activities virtually confined to one school (Jespersen). Purely receptive activities were rare, and communicative writing activities were completely absent from the corpus. Secondly, the topics of discourse during communicative FL segments were largely restricted to the phatic and the instrumental. Very few communicative FL activities had a dominant informational purpose or involved the acquisition of new skills by pupils.

The obverse of this pattern can be seen, if the relatively rare English medium segments identified in these lessons are contrasted with the communicative FL segments. Such things as role plays, games, or guessing activities, never took place through the medium of English. On the other hand, the giving of information about the French way of life typically did so. While not all teachers provided metalinguistic information for their pupils (teacher opinion being apparently divided as to whether the provision of grammatical 'explanations' is of any use to 12 and 13-year-old learners, as might have been expected from the relevant Stage 1 interview data reported in Chapter 3, those who did so used English for the purpose without exception. 'Skill training' (e.g. how to read a map or timetable), if it proved necessary, almost always took place through English (with one exception noted at Sweet), and all discussions of unit objectives did so too. Lastly, any more than superficial discussion of real life issues (e.g. 'Should World War II still influence our attitude to the Germans?': Palmer), while rare, entailed a switch to English even in classrooms with high, stable levels of French usage.

Thus it appeared that any activities involving the introduction of substantial new information, concepts or skills were likely to take place in English, as were activities requiring a substantial, non-routine linguistic contribution from pupils. Indeed, there seemed to be a generally shared assumption among teachers that using a new language constitutes a substantial cognitive load for the learner, and that the content of communicative FL discourse should therefore be kept as 'light' as possible. Additionally, it seemed that teachers anticipated a substantial increase in communication difficulties, if things such as the transmission of significant new or abstract information, or lengthy open-ended discussion, were attempted via the FL.

Constraints on 'personal' discussion

It was also a very general feature of these lessons that while personal/affective topics were very popular subjects for communicative FL segments, these were almost always treated at a fairly superficial level (in spite of the relaxed atmosphere and generally good teacher-pupil relations which seemed to prevail in these classrooms). Such activities typically entailed no more than the exchange of basic information about families, pets, hobbies, etc, or the bald expressions of likes and dislikes about school subjects, food, etc, with little encouragement for individuals to develop, qualify, or justify their opinions.

Two possible explanations for such limited treatment of 'personal' topics suggested themselves: one had to do with the avoidance of linguistic difficulties and the generation of possible unmanageable demands on the limited language resources of the pupils, the other with constraints deriving from the formal class-room setting and the social roles of 'teacher' and 'pupils' required of participants therein.

The role of the competent FL speaker

In most 'real life' contexts in which the learner is likely to use an FL in oral interaction, his/her interlocutors will be native speakers of the language. That is, those with whom he/she interacts are likely (a) normally to provide 'correct' models of FL usage in their own speech, and (b) to have a sufficient repertoire of communication skills to be in a position to help the learner both to understand what is said to him/her, and to express what he/she wants to say.

In the FL classroom only one person, the teacher, is normally sufficiently competent in the target language to support the learner in this way. The context is the opposite of that in which informal acquisition usually happens; while in 'real life' many fluent speakers interact with individual learners, in the classroom one fluent speaker faces many learners. To find the best use of this scarce 'resource' of fluency is therefore vitally important.

The teachers observed for this study adopted somewhat different strategies of 'self-deployment' during communicative FL activities, each seeming to have its own advantages and problems from this point of view. Some teachers ran such segments on a whole-class basis, themselves interacting with different members of the class in turn, with the rest listening/waiting their turn. This strategy ensured that the selected individuals in turn received directly (and in a few classrooms, sometimes for several minutes each), the benefits of interaction with a fluent FL speaker. For the rest of the class, however, this was a vicarious experience, which seemed at times to involve them only minimally. For instance, it sometimes appeared difficult for the teacher to take enough time to assist an individual to express what he/she wanted to say, while keeping sufficient 'momentum' in the discussion as a whole to sustain the interest of the rest of the pupils.

Several other teachers on the other hand favoured pairs and small groups as the organisational forms for most interactive communicative FL activities. After launching an activity of this type, they would circulate among the pupils, joining individual pairs/groups for anything up to several minutes at a time. Like the previous one, this strategy also affords opportunities to individual pupils for spells of direct interaction with a competent FL speaker. For most of the time, however, they are attempting communicative FL interaction with other learners. The great advantage of this pattern is of course that far more pupils should be actively engaged in communicative FL performance at any one moment; however, learners can neither rely on each other as correct models of FL usage, nor support each others' attempts to speak as fluent speakers could. Partly for these reasons, pupil-pupil communicative FL activities occasionally broke down altogether; such activities also sometimes appeared to be a source of at least temporary confusion concerning formal aspects of the FL language system. This form of organisation also seems to demand some special skills of the teacher; the capacity to monitor the level of activity in the class generally while interacting with a single pair or group, and the capacity to distribute attention 'fairly' around the class, perhaps over a period of days, both seem necessary.

CHAPTER 3

ACTION RESEARCH STUDIES I: ROLE PLAY AND SIMULATION

DEFINITIONS OF ROLE PLAY AND SIMULATION

The terms 'role play' and 'simulation' are used widely in the literature of education and psychology, with varying definitions.

In this study we used both terms to apply to activities in which pairs or groups of pupils (or pupil(s) and teacher) enacted an entire imaginary speech event. 'Role play' was used for activities in which at least some participants took the part of 'characters' other than their real selves (such as waiters, policemen or pen pal family members); 'simulation' was used for activities in which participants kept their own identities, but enacted an imaginary situation (e.g. arranging an outing with a friend).

Role plays and simulations are both to be distinguished from structure drills and exercises by their character as complete speech events, with discourse coherence obtaining (or at least being aimed at) throughout the entire activity. Their interest for FL teaching and learning lies of course in the wider experience of target language use which it is felt such activities can provide. They can systematically and economically introduce the learner to a wide range of situations in which he/she may expect to get involved in real life language use. Exponents for the range of language functions likely to be required can be introduced more or less 'naturally', and repeated enactment of a given situation, with appropriate variations, can be expected to consolidate and develop the learner's language resource and his/her flexibility in accessing it, as well as boosting his/her confidence and readiness to speak. Perhaps most importantly, the face validity, and consequent motivating power, of such activities for learners appear to be strong.

THE COMMUNICATIVE/PRACTICE DISTINCTION WITHIN ROLE PLAY

As we saw in Chapter 1 many teachers seem to take it for granted that oral interactive activities of the role play type provide pupils with experience of communicative FL use. However, according to the definition of communicative language use adopted for this project, no such assumption can be made. It is perfectly possible to conceive of 'lets pretend' activities which have the rehearsal of preselected formal language items as their main or sole purpose.

For example, the pre-scripted situational dialogue, which has an old and honourable place in L2 teaching, meets criteria being suggested here for role play, consisting as it usually does of an entire imaginary speech event. However, the uses made of such dialogues in audiovisual/audiolingual methodology (repetition, memorisation and exact reproduction) fail to meet the 'unpredictability' criterion for communicative FL use.

To count as a 'communicative' activity, then, a role play or simulation must meet certain conditions. Not only must a context and a purpose for language use be proposed, and roles suggested about which participants have, or can acquire, relevant social knowledge. (In simulations these roles of course remain participants' own selves.) Additionally, language use must be appropriate to the specified context, roles and purpose, unpredictable, and coherent. Communicative role plays are those which will both draw upon, and hopefully develop, the full range of participants' linguistic and social knowledge and their interactive skills (e.g. turntaking and the ability to effect 'repairs' in the event of breakdown in communication, as well as grammar, vocabulary etc).

ROLE PLAY AND THE OBSERVATIONAL VISITS

As we saw in Chapter 2 role play and simulation activities as defined above were relatively uncommon in most of the classrooms initially observed for Stage 2. The teachers commonly provided some context even for tightly structured practice FL exercises rehearsing functionally related exponents. However, such activities do not meet the 'coherence' criterion of fully fledged role play; and indeed the teachers themselves claimed no more than that contextualisation provided a humanising (and hopefully motivating) lead into practice FL activity. Activities that they (and the Communicative Interaction Project criteria) recognised as fully fledged role plays or simulations were 'special events' in all classrooms but one.

Within the general category of role play/simulation, both practice and communicative activities were observed, as we have also seen in Chapter 2. While the improvisational character of the majority of role play activities meant that they met 'communicative criteria', instances also occurred of the reading aloud or memorisation and enactment of entirely pre-scripted (and therefore entirely predictable) dialogues.

The views reported in Chapter 1 make it plain that many teachers see role play activities with an improvisational aspect (i.e. communicative role play) as something to be undertaken towards the end of any given learning unit, providing pupils with an opportunity to put together and re-combine a range of newly-learned target language items, which have initially been practised separately. This perception of the proper time for creative role play activity seemed to be shared by many of the teachers observed in Stage 2. Thus, in most classrooms a range of more or less analytic, practice FL activities were the main learning experiences provided at the segmental level, with integrative communicative activities such as creative role play occurring only intermittently, as occasions for re-use of material previously mastered. Only one teacher out of the original thirteen made communicative role play and simulation activities the predominant element in his pupils' learning experience, using them if not for the very first introduction of new language material, at least for early familiarisation and consolidation.

These different patterns of occurrence of improvisational role play activity can be related to different theoretical models of L2 learning. The commoner pattern, in which role play occurred at the end of a chain of successively more open teaching/learning activities, can be accounted for in terms of the traditional or stages theory (Hatch, 1978), according to which new language items must first be learned separately, and then integrated systematically into the learner's developing language system, before it makes sense to attempt creative L2 use. The minority pattern, in which creative FL use was encouraged regularly throughout any given unit of work, comes closer to realising newer theories which suggest that even in classrooms, unconscious acquisition through direct experience of communicative language use is a key process in developing L2 competence, perhaps even more important than step-by-step learning (Krashen, 1982).

ROLE PLAY AND SIMULATION: OVERVIEW OF ACTION RESEARCH STUDIES

During the return visits of Stage 2, one or two teachers in each school agreed to run a role play or simulation activity as the focus of an action research study. Four role play and two simulation studies were completed. Three role play studies were carried out at S1 level; the remaining role play, and both simulation studies, were carried out in S2.

In each case, at least two preliminary interviews were held with the teacher concerned, firstly to define in broad terms the activity to be undertaken, and secondly to document the teacher's fully developed plans for the activity, to agree procedures for collecting data concerning the actual implementation of the activity, and to clarify criteria by which the activity would initially be evaluated.

The actual teaching in all cases remained the business of the class teacher. Where the opportunity arose the activity was carried out with more than one class. In all but two cases (Role Plays 3 and 4), the activities which were the focus of study were completed within a single lesson. After some form of whole-class introduction, all the activities were run on a paired or group basis. The researcher was present throughout as an observer, with the responsibility of audiorecording as much as possible of the proceedings. In all cases the teacher wore a radiomicrophone which allowed for a complete audiorecording of his/her interaction with the whole class, with groups, or with individuals. Several portable cassette recorders were used to record pupil-pupil interaction in pairs or groups. In two studies (Role Play 2 and Simulation 2) all pupils were recorded. In the rest, only a sample of pupil performance was obtained; however, this sample was randomly selected and included a majority of the pupils in every case.

After the activity had been completed, an attempt was made in most cases to document pupils' reactions to it. This was done by the researcher, either by the immediate administration of a simple written questionnaire to the whole class (as in Role Play 2 and Simulation 2) or by interviewing selected pairs or groups of pupils, as opportunity offered, over the next few days (using playback of their own recorded performance to stimulate recall). Finally, a 'post-mortem' interview was held with the teacher to gather his/her perceptions of how the activity had gone, and to conduct an initial joint evaluation of it. These discussions with the teacher were also lent focus either by replay of selected portions of the recorded material, or by consideration of transcripts if already prepared.

Subsequent to this school-based phase, the researcher completed the business of transcribing both the whole-class, teacher-led introductions to the various activities, and the recordings of the actual role play/simulation work. Papers giving accounts of the studies were produced and circulated to all participating teachers. The following sections of this chapter describing the studies in more detail are based on these reports.

Role Play 1

SUMMARY DESCRIPTION

The first role play study was carried out in the second term of S1. At the end of a unit or work in which relevant language had been taught (*Tour de France* Stage I, *Le beau Paris*), Teacher D turned her S1 mixed ability classroom into a *café* for one 40-minute period. All 24 pupils present were simultaneously involved in this role play activity; groups of 'customers' sat around *café* tables and were served by 'waiters', who took orders and served food and drink which they collected from a 'bar' at one end of the room (at which 'servers' were in attendance). The food and drinks were represented by mini-flashcards the pupils had previously made, and pupils had quantities of paper 'money' with which to pay the bill.

The teacher managed the entire lesson (including explaining the task, allocating roles and distributing realia) almost exclusively through French, without encountering any obvious difficulties. The role play activity occupied the entire lesson. It was introduced by two model conversations enacted for the whole class by a group of several pupils plus the teacher. These models were unrehearsed, impromptu affairs. The teacher began the first model with a minimum of explanation, summoning individuals to her own desk:

TD   *.... Bon alors, il y a quatre chaises ici. Geneviève, assieds-toi là, s'il te plaît. Henri, assieds-toi là. Gilbert, assieds-toi là. Gilbert. Et Mathieu, s'il te plaît, assieds-toi là. .... Ehh bon alors, qui veut être le garçon ici? Ça c'est un bar, oui? Ça c'est le bar dans le café. Qui veut être le garçon? Jacques, toi? Alors assieds-toi là - ah non, mets-toi là. Bon alors, tout le monde écoutez bien. Ici, c'est une table dans mon café. Moi je suis le garçon. Bonjour monsieur, mademoiselle!*

PP   *Bonjour, monsieur*

TD   *Alors, qu'est-ce que vous prenez?*

P1   *Un sandwich et une coca, s'il vous plaît*
TD   *Un sandwich, oui, et un coca?*
P1   *Oui*
TD   *Oui, monsieur?*
P2   *Un bière et ... un glace, s'il te plaît*
TD   *Une bière et une glace, oui. Une bière... et une glace. A la fraise ou à la vanille?*
P1   *La vanille*
TD   *A la vanille, oui. Mademoiselle?*
P3   *Un café un - un lait, s'il te plaît*
TD   *Un café au lait, oui. C'est tout?*
P3   *Oui*
TD   *Oui? Oui, monsieur?* (etc)

During this first model the teacher played a waiter; during the second, she played a customer. She sustained her roles consistently apart from issuing brief practical instructions and introducing a necessary language item:

TD   *Bon alors, vous buvez, vous mangez!*
         (sound effects)
P1   *J'adore le coca!*
TD   *Bon alors, maintenant if faut payer, oui? Il faut payer. Alors qu'est-ce que vous dites? Vous dites, 'L'addition s'il vous plaît'. 'L'addition', qu'est-ce que c'est, 'l'addition'?*
PP   The bill?
TD   *Oui, Henri?*
P1   The bill
TD   The bill, *oui, c'est ça. L'addition.* (writes 'l'addition' on blackboard) *'L'addition', ça c'est* 'the bill'. *L'addition'*
P1   *Pardon!*
TD   *Oui, monsieur?*
P1   *L'addition, s'il vous plaît* (etc)

Between the two models, and after them, the teacher gave detailed activity instructions in French. Once the pupil groups themselves embarked on the activity, she played a supervisory role, helping with practical problems and individual language needs where necessary:

P1   I'm going to ask how to say "There's a tip". *Comment est-ce qu'on - comment est-ce qu'on dit,* 'a tip'? .... Miss! Miss!
TD   *Oui?*

P1   Miss, *comment est-ce qu'on dit,* 'a tip'? 'Here's a tip'?
TD   *'Un pourboire', 'un pourboire'* (etc) (Group 4, first attempt)

The activity was carried out twice, with pupils remaining in the same groups but swapping roles between attempts. There were seven pupil groups altogether; intelligible audiorecordings were obtained for five out of the seven, and these were used as a basis for retrospective discussions with the pupil groups.

PUPIL PERFORMANCE

This activity elicited high levels of pupil interest and involvement, which were sustained throughout the lesson. The transcripts of the recorded groups run from five to nine pages; they show that all groups clearly understood what was required, and completed the various 'transactional' stages of the activity at least once. All groups followed the broad outlines of the model conversations fairly closely, and the still limited nature of the pupils' French language resource is revealed in the lack of variety of exponents for certain key transactional functions as well as in the considerable number of minor morphological errors. However, the transcribed conversations all clearly met the criteria for a communicative speech event - purpose, coherence, unpredictability, etc. The overall impression is one of spontaneity and inventiveness in exploiting a limited language resource, as the following excerpts show:

(Ordering)

TD   (to whole class) *Okay, à table!*
P   (waitress) *Bonjour, mademoiselle*
P2   *Bonjour, madame*
P3   *Bonjour, madame*
P4   *Un coca, s'il te plaît. Et une vin blanc. Pardon, c'est combien ce coca grand?*
P1   *Six - c'est six francs*
P4   *C'est six francs! Non, non, ce coca, non. C'est combien le vin blanc?*
P1   *C'est quatre*
P4   *C'est quatre francs?*
P1   *Oui, merci*
P4   *Emm, ce vin blanc et un chocolat, s'il te - s'il vous plaît....*
P1   *Merci*
P2   *Une sandwich et une glace -*

P1	(writing) *Minute*
P2	*- et une café*
P1	*Sandwich, une glace, une café* (etc) (Group 5, second attempt)
	(Getting served & playing)
P1	*Où est le garçon? Ah bon*
P2	(waiter, arrives with tray) *Un coca?*
P3	*Oui, c'est pour moi, merci*
P2	*Une bière. (....) deux bières*
P1	*Ah moi, c'est pour qui - moi. Merci*
P2	*Un vin rouge?*
P1	*C'est pour moi, merci*
P2	*Un gateau?*
P4	*C'est pour moi, merci*
P1	*Et l'addition, s'il te plaît ....*
P2	*Une bière, six francs*
P1	*(....) six francs*
P2	*Un vin rouge, cinq francs*
P1	(counting money) *Deux, deux .... deux. Et bière?*
P2	*Bière est six francs, vin rouge cinq francs*
P1	*Cinq francs. Deux, deux, et un. Oui?*
P2	*Merci* (etc) (Group 3, first attempt)

Several groups went beyond their original brief in unexpected ways. Notably, two recorded groups carried out some ancillary managerial activity (allocating roles, sharing out fake money) at least partly through the target language, without any explicit directions to this effect:

(Money shareout)

P1	(Money is being dealt out) *Merci, merci*
P2	*Merci*
P3	*Oh, je n'ai pas de cinq francs!*
P4	*Je n'ai pas de un franc!*
P3	*Un franc? Moi, c'est deux un francs, deux*
P1	(adding up total) *Vingt-et-un (....)!*
P2	*(....)*
P1	*Vingt-et-un francs! ....* (etc) (Group 5, between attempts)

This extension of FL use to managerial topics for which exponents have not systematically been taught led to some decline in formal accuracy, contrasting with the level of language of the actual role plays. But pupils' willingness to sustain FL use in this way was nonetheless remarkable.

At least two groups also exceeded their 'brief' in the course of the activity, by engaging in general social conversation in French between the visits of the waiter (and incidentally displaying some skill in conversational repair). For example:

(Waiter is fetching order)

P1	*Tais-toi. Quel âge as-tu, Danielle? Quel âge as-tu?*
P2	*Je m'appelle Danielle*
P1 }	*Quel âge as-tu?*
P3 }	
P2	*J'ai douze ans*
P1	*Tu as douze ans?*
P2	*Non - J'ai treize ans!*
P1	*Tu as treize ans? Moi, c'est douze ans*
P3	*Moi aussi*
P1	*Tu as douze ans? Tu as onze ans?*
P3	*Douze ans*
P1	*Douze ans?*
P3	*Oui*
P2	*J'ai treize ans. C'est maman - bon* anniversary
P1	*Pardon?*
P2	*C'est - moi maman -* anniversary!
P1	*Ahh! C'est maman* anniversary?
P2	*Oui*
P1	*Je comprends* (etc) (Group 5, second attempt)

This possibility was only hinted at in the preliminary model conversations, but seemed to arise naturally from the realistic staging of the activity, given the requirement that waiters collect actual materials from another part of the room, thus creating suitable pauses.

PUPIL REACTIONS

Due to poor recording quality it was not possible to analyse in detail the retrospective group discussions held with the pupils. However, these discussions made it clear that the activity had substantial face validity among pupils. Notably, the physical as well as verbal enactment of the situation, and the manipulation of objects, were mentioned as adding realism to the situation, and encouraging appropriate language use.

Role Play 2

SUMMARY DESCRIPTION

The second role play study involved Teacher H at Bloomfield High School. It was again conducted at S1 level, this time in the third term of the school year. Teacher H was responsible for two mixed ability S1 classes, and carried out the role play activity in a similar way with both classes.

The chosen activity was based on a *Tour de France* Stage 1 'compound language task', and was carried out at the end of a unit of work in which relevant language material had been taught. Both classes did the activity on the same day; in each case the activity filled an entire hour-long lesson. 25 pupils were present for one session, 28 for the other.

The supposed setting for the role play was a French school canteen; the pupils were seated at 'canteen tables', in groups of four to six to which they were assigned by the teacher. Within each group one child adopted the role of a newly-arrived Scottish teenage visitor; the rest were his/her French hosts. Five successive role play scenes were enacted within the overall framework: 1. Introductions; 2. Showing photos; 3. Discussing the menu; 4. Having the meal; and 5. Touring the school.

In this case, the activity was managed mainly through English. After a general L1 introduction, the first scene was modelled twice for the whole class, first by a group including the teacher (role playing the Scottish visitor) and then by an all-pupil group. (This was done on an impromptu basis, without any prior revision of relevant language material.) After modelling, all pupil groups simultaneously enacted the first scene. When they had finished, scenes 2-4 were successively treated in the same way (improvised modelling, followed by simultaneous enactment). Lastly, scene 5 was enacted by selected pairs only, with the rest of the pupils as audience.

The overall purpose of the interaction was clearly affective/phatic, unlike the more narrowly transactional Role Play 1. The teacher roughly sketched out one possible scenario:

TH   *(....) We want it to be quite normal, for instance when you meet people for the first time, 'Hullo. What's your name?*

What age are you? Where do you live? How are you? Do you have brothers and sisters?' etc.

This outline was broadly followed in the first model conversation.

However, such suggestions for conversational sequencing of utterances obviously had a different status from those necessarily entailed in the café scene of Role Play 1 (where, minimally, the functions of ordering, being served, and paying the bill had to be accomplished, and in a particular order, for the speech event to appear both coherent and complete). If available language resources allowed, a looser conversational structure, and greater variation between groups, might be expected.

Additionally, the task selected for Role Play 2 was making greater imaginative demands of the pupil. The teacher encouraged them to 'imagine yourselves that you're not Scottish people any more, but that you're French'; it became clear that rather more detailed French 'personalities' would be required than was the case for Role Play 1. The pupils found this out by trial and error to some extent, in the model conversations:

TH	*Quel quel âge as-tu, Michel?*
P1	*J'ai douze ans*
TH	*Ah, douze ans, et toi?*
P2	*J'ai treize ans*
TH	*Treize ans, ah oui. Où habites-tu?*
P2	*J'habite à* (names real home town*) - oh!*
TH	*Ah non, 'j'habite à ...'*
P2	*Montan* (appropriate French location)
TH	*A Montan, ah oui? Très bien! Et toi Michel, où habites-tu?*
	(etc) (Scene 1, first model)

But some confusion of real, and imaginary, personal details seemed to persist:

TH	*(....) Et toi Lynn, tu as des soeurs?*
P2	*Oui*
TH	*Ah oui? Combien de soeurs?*
P2	*J'ai deux*
TH	*Deux soeurs? Comment s'appellent-elles?*
P2	*Elles s'appellent Jackie 'n Angela*
TH	*Elles s'appellent Jacqueline et Angèle, très bien* (etc) (Scene 1, first model)

PUPIL PERFORMANCE

This activity also evoked and sustained high levels of pupil involvement. All groups grasped the requirements of the task, and without prior rehearsal produced lively and original conversations on the lines of the impromptu models. There were some false starts, however, for instance where the distinctive role of 'Scottish visitor' was taken by a pupil with limited competence in French; once or twice the reallocation of this role was necessary before conversations could get off the ground.

The first of the five 'scenes' will be discussed in some detail. All groups covered all or most of the conversation topics suggested by the teacher for this scene: names, ages, siblings, etc. Almost all groups also dealt with two other topics, at greater or lesser length: ownership of pets, and likes and dislikes (regarding school subjects, and/or hobbies, food, and drink). Thus the pupils stuck overall to topics for which the *Tour de France* Stage 1 syllabus had prepared them.

Members of several groups had some difficulty in consistently sustaining their roles - 'French' roles in particular. For example, 'French children' supposedly attending the same school sometimes failed to coordinate their individual stories:

P1 (Scot) *Où habites-tu?*
P2 *J'habite à Montan*
P3 *J'habite à Créteil*
P4 *J'habite à Paris*
P5 *J'habite à Paris* (etc) (Group 5/am)

Others drifted back into their own real life Scottish character as their conversation progressed:

P1 (Scot), (...), *tu as un frère, tu as une soeur?*
P2 *Oui, j'ai deux frères, j'ai deux soeurs*
P1 *Comment s'appellent-ils?*
P2 *Elles* (sic) *s'appellent John et Kerry*
P1 *Comment s'appellent-elles?*
P2 *Elles s'appellent Elaine et Anne* (etc) (Group 5/pm)

One group ended up discussing (still in French) their preferences among teachers in their own real-life school.

The discourse structure of the group conversations on the whole reflected a good understanding on the pupils' part of how such conversations might go in real life. In some respects, however, the constraints of the situation, in which groups clearly felt obliged to keep on generating talk, plus the limitations of the language resource available to participants, led to distortions in the discourse structure. Firstly, the distribution of speech turns among participants was remarkably even for all groups. This seemed to arise from a generally shared understanding that all group members should provide similar information about themselves (this was indeed implied in the preliminary models, though not explicitly stated). This often led to somewhat repetitive Q/A sequences (if necessary, as here, weaker group members were prompted so as to carry this through):

P1	(Scot) *(...) Où habites-tu, Michel?*
P2	*J'habite à Créteil, en France*
P1	*Et toi, Fiona?*
P3	*J'habite à Paris, en France*
P1	*Et toi, Anne-Marie?*
P4	*J'habite à Paris, en France*
P5	*J'habite à Paris, en France*
P1	*Et toi, Marc? ...*
P2	(prompting) *J'habite à Créteil*
P6	*J'habite à Créteil*
P1	*En France?*
P6	*Oui, et toi? ...*
P1	*Emm, j'habite à* (home town), *en Ecosse* (etc) (Group 5/pm)

Once the topic of discussion shifted beyond the opening gambits of name/age/domicile, these repetitive, round-the-table sequences usually disappeared. However, they were sometimes replaced by strings of semi-autonomous Q/A exchanges, with only the most general topical coherence:

P1	(Scot) *Tu aimes les maths, Robert?*
P2	*Non, non, je déteste les maths*
P1	*André, tu aimes l'anglais?*
P3	*Eh, comme ça*
P1	*Eileen, tu aimes la gymnastique?*
P4	*Oui, j'adore la gymnastique* (etc) (Group 4/am)

In this example, the structural resemblance between successive exchanges is more striking than their coherence as discourse.

However, all conversations included structurally differentiated, topically coherent sequences at least some of the time:

P1   (Scot) *Tu as une animal à la maison?*
P2   *(...)*
P3   *Huit animals* (sic) *à la maison!*
P1   *Tu aimes les animals?*
P3   *Oui, j'adore... animals* (etc) (Group 5/am)

Despite these oddities of discourse structure, the overall impression was of the pupils as fairly accomplished conversation-makers, exploiting still very limited language resources to produce lively and plausible conversations. However, one thing many groups did fail to do was to bring their conversations to any definite conclusion.

TEACHER RETROSPECTIVE COMMENT

Teacher H was generally pleased with the level of pupil involvement and the quality of interaction produced. Though he was aware of some structural repetitiveness, lack of topical development, and lack of flexibility in turntaking, he felt the level of performance was creditable for S1 pupils on such an open-ended and unstructured task. He stressed the importance of group formation for activities of this type; pupils had been carefully allocated to ensure a balance of both sex and ability.

PUPIL REACTIONS

Pupil reactions to the activity were gauged by means of a written questionnaire. Of the 52 pupils who filled it in, 26 agreed that their conversation was 'like real life', while 22 disagreed (the rest held qualified views). Those who disagreed gave a variety of reasons: twelve pupils mentioned some inappropriacy of the topics discussed to the situation ('You wouldn't talk about those things over dinner'); eight mentioned inappropriacy in matters of form ('You wouldn't ask so many questions'), and others mentioned lack of fluency ('French people would speak more fluently and with an accent'), nervousness and selfconsciousness among participants ('You were all tense with a mic in front of you').

Asked which role was easier to play, a large majority said it was easier to be a French person than a Scottish person (39 pupils)! However, the most popular reasons given for choosing one over the other had to do with the type of participation expected. Twelve pupils thought the easier roles were those which had less to say (in this case the French roles), and seventeen thought it was easier to have a responding rather than an initiating role ('The French people just answered the things the Scottish person was saying'). However, eight pupils thought initiation was easier ('It was easier giving the questions').

Strikingly, only four pupils seemed to take account of 'social knowledge' problems involved in taking on a role ('I think it was easier to play a Scottish person because I am Scottish'). Seven pupils argued the situation was easier for the French person 'because French people are used to speaking French' - that is, apparently reinterpreting the question to consider the actual situation in France, rather than the role play, classroom version.

35 pupils (including many playing 'French' characters) also agreed with the statement that 'I was trying to say what was true', while only eighteen agreed that 'I was trying to make things up to fit the situation'. 37 and 30 respectively agreed that they were trying to 'speak as much French as possible' and 'say things I can say in French'. Thus out of these four statements, the only one with which a majority disagreed was that to do with 'making things up'.

The last question asked pupils how well they felt they could cope in a real French dinner hall, and what problems they would expect. Pupils responded thoughtfully and realistically, anticipating problems with comprehension, speaking (especially vocabulary), the speed with which French people talk, and (in one class) their own ignorance of French slang (!). Nonetheless, in each class a narrow majority felt they could cope, at least some of the time.

Role Play 3

SUMMARY DESCRIPTION

The third role play study was conducted with an S2 class at Bloomfield High School, in their third term. In this case the pupils were told several days in advance that they were going to act out a market scene. The necessary language resource was rehearsed, including the introduction of some new material pertinent to prices; stallholder roles were also allocated ahead of time. Two preceding sessions were devoted to the making of materials (money, signs, and cutout fruits, fish, etc); this activity was managed largely through English.

On the day the role play scene was carried out, eighteen pupils were present. 'Stallholders' manned stalls dispersed around the classroom (for vegetables, fruit, icecream, groceries, fish, delicatessen, and wine). The stalls were stocked with a mixture of realia (packets, cartons, etc) and the cutout drawings made by the pupils. The remaining pupils were issued with shopping bags, money, and cards bearing a brief character summary (e.g. 'housewife with young children', 'Monitrice, shopping for a picnic'), and blank shopping lists. The customers wrote out their own shopping lists, appropriate to their given character. The teacher herself modelled the scene once, visiting a stall and playing customer while the pupils watched:

TF	Now first of all... I am going to pretend, okay? To give you an idea of what is expected of you, I am going to pretend that I am a customer, right? I'm a housewife, I've got ten children at home, and I've got to go shopping for them. Now, I go along to the market, not knowing exactly what is going to be available. And I don't know either how the stall holders are feeling, what they are going to say to me and so on. So I have got to be on my toes, and to make sure that I can carry out the conversation with them. Right? *(...) Mmm, bonjour monsieur*
P1	*Bonjour madame*
TF	*Ça va aujourd'hui?*
P1	*(...) ...et vous?*
TF	*Et vous. Il fait beau aujourd'hui, n'est-ce pas? Il fait beau aujourd'hui... Oui? Ou non?*
P1	*Oui*
TF	*Oui, il fait très beau. D'accord. Emm, excusez-moi, qu'est-ce que c'est, ça? Qu'est-ce que c'est, ça?*
P1	*C'est cinq francs*
TF	*Ecoutez, s'il vous plaît! Qu'est-ce que c'est, ça? Qu'est-ce que c'est? C'est... une sardine? C'est du thon? Qu'est-ce que c'est?*
P1	*C'est un poisson*
TF	*C'est un poisson?* (laughs) *Mais; c'est emm... une sole? Une sole?*
P1	Haddock
TF	*Non? C'est du haddock? D'accord, c'est du haddock. Alors, un kilo de haddock s'il vous plaît monsieur, un kilo de haddock.* Now, pretend you've got a weighing-machine somewhere. *Un kilo de haddock... Ehh très bien. Vous l'enveloppez, s'il vous plaît?*

P1	*Oui*
TF	*Vous l'enveloppez, merci...*
P1	(wraps haddock) *Voulez-vous autre chose?*
TF	*Alors ehh, le - le haddock, c'est combien s'il vous plaît?*
P1	*C'est sept francs*
TF	*C'est sept francs, très bien, sept francs. Et je voudrais aussi, je voudrais ehh des moules, des moules. Alors, deux kilos de moules, s'il vous plaît*
P1	*C'est -*
TF	*Deux kilos de moules, s'il vous plaît. C'est combien, les moules? c'est combien?*
P1	*Trent francs*
TF	*Le kilo? C'est cher! Trent francs le kilo!*
P1	*Non -*
TF	*Oh là là, c'est cher, hein?*
P1	*Non, emm, quinze francs un kilo*
TF	*Très bien, quinze francs, quinze francs le kilo. D'accord. Deux kilos, s'il vous plaît. Deux kilos de moules. Ça va... Il est frais, le poisson? Il est frais?* What do you think I'm asking?
P2	Is it fresh?
TF	*Il est frais, oui?*
P1	*Oui*
TF	*Aujourd'hui?*
P1	*Oui*
TF	*Très bien, bravo. Mm, ça sent bon, le poisson. Il sent très bon... D'accord. Et aussi, je voudrais une livre, une livre de sardines, s'il vous plaît. C'est combien, les sardines? C'est combien?... C'est combien?*
P1	*(...) ... (...)* did you want? Is it -
TF	No, I said, *C'est combien, les sardines?*
P1	*Emm, c'est... Vingt-cinq francs*
TF	*Vingt-cinq francs? Le kilo? Le kilo. Alors, une livre de sardines. Une livre de sardines, s'il vous plaît. Ehh, mes moules, oui c'est à moi ça, merci...* (P1 wraps sardines with mussels) *Ah, avec les moules. D'accord, avec les moules! Très bien. Merci monsieur. Alors c'est combien, s'il vous plaît?* ...Let's make it fifteen, or ten, or - oh, I've got no money! *(...) Alors c'est combien, s'il vous plaît? C'est combien?*
P1	*C'est... quarante-neuf francs*
TF	*Voilà monsieur. Quarante-neuf ...cinquante. Je vous remercie monsieur. Au revoir monsieur*
P1	*Au revoir*
TF	*A demain, à demain monsieur.* All right, so you get the idea... (etc)

This model conversation shows Teacher F switching into English for some practical instructions and in sorting out comprehension difficulties, as well as for the general introduction to the activity. However, these incidents apart, the appropriate roles were generally sustained, and the model clearly indicated the improvisational nature of the intended activity, and encouraged pupils to go beyond strictly transactional language use in customer-stallholder interaction.

The various introductory preliminaries, including enactment of the model, took c. 30 minutes; the scene itself, with all 'customers' shopping simultaneously, queuing,etc, lasted for fifteen minutes.

PUPIL COMMENTS

On the day following the activity, ten 'customers' were interviewed in pairs about their experience of the activity. They all reported having done some preparatory revision and claimed that this had been helpful. Most said they had visited about five stalls, but had not completed their shopping, due to shortage of time. They had been flexible in their shopping, substituting other items if what they asked for was not available. They said the stallholders had not attempted to give correct change, however; most customers 'did not bother' about this, while two boys who said they had insisted on getting the correct change both reported resorting to English to do so.

The pupils varied in their estimation of the 'realism' of the activity. However, all agreed it had been useful and/or enjoyable; several mentioned that acting things out helps develop confidence, and all agreed that having props to manipulate meant that 'it felt more real'.

PUPIL PERFORMANCE

Direct observation tallied with the pupils' comments in suggesting pupils found the activity both enjoyable and involving. (The teacher was gratified at the sustained level of purposeful activity; she was particularly pleased with the level of involvement of the poorer pupils - 'There is something in it for everyone'.) The proportion of language use to non-verbal 'business' in pupil-pupil interaction was, however, rather low (by comparison with the activities previously described), and pupils mostly stuck to the narrowly transactional exchanges of buying and selling, in spite of wider initial modelling by the teacher. (This was, however, the pupils' first attempt at so open-ended an activity.)

The balance between time spent by the pupils preparing for this activity (two and a half sessions) seemed rather disproportionate to that spent actually doing it (half a session), especially given the mainly English-medium character of this preliminary preparation. The teacher however felt sufficiently positive about the experience to consider building similar activities more regularly into her pupils' classroom experience.

Role Play 4

SUMMARY DESCRIPTION

The three role play studies previously described involved group interaction among pupils, with the teacher in a supervisory and 'prompting' role, after initial modelling had taken place. The fourth study afforded an opportunity to study teacher behaviour in the course of role play activity.

At the time of the return visit, in term 2, to Palmer High School, Teacher B was engaged in testing her S2 class. It was realised that this test material could be used to shed extra light on 'communicative' role plays, as the test involved among other things the enactment of paired role play scenes between the teacher and individual pupils. Over a series of lessons, therefore, eighteen pupils were recorded taking the test (thirteen boys and five girls); each pupil engaged in a minimum of three role play scenes with the teacher.

On-the-spot test management, including presentation of the 'scenarios' for the role play conversations, took place in French; there was no preliminary modelling. However, pupils had previously received a printed 'information sheet' listing the twelve possible scenarios, and had been encouraged to revise and to rehearse the conversations with other pupils.

The topics of conversation varied from the narrowly transactional (*dans la rue: 'agent'/'touriste'*) to the more open and social (*au port: 'vieux pêcheur'/'touriste'*). The teacher always played the French character, the pupil a tourist or visitor. The test framework required that pupils produce at least four utterances; the teacher was expected to score pupil performance concurrently with test administration.

TEACHER COMMENTARY

Teacher B had a number of comments to make about this type of role play activity. She felt that the performance of several different role plays in immediate succession was confusing for less able/less extrovert pupils. Fuller contextualisation, including the provision of realia, and the provision of a 'few ideas' on what to say would also have helped pupils put themselves in context. It was hard for them to accept the teacher in some roles (e.g. playing the part of another pupil).

Teacher B also commented that the situations varied in 'difficulty'; she felt pupils found those with an obvious transactional purpose easier to handle than more open, 'social' situations. Situations involving comment and discussion about third parties were also perceived as harder, partly because third person forms had been less thoroughly mastered, partly because an extra effort of imagination was required.

The teacher, as the 'adult native speaker', played a leading role in all the recorded conversations. Asked to comment on her own decision-making as the conversations progressed, concerning what topics to introduce, and how to respond to what pupils said, she made it clear that her behaviour was not random, but calculated to maximise the chances of a coherent conversation being produced. Thus she spoke of introducing topics for discussion for which she knew a basic language resource should be available (and occasionally steered pupils who introduced 'divergent' topics back in the direction of coursebook material). This accounted for much of the family resemblance noticeable between role play conversations and coursebook dialogues. However, these family resemblances did not at any point involve the exact rehearsal of previously memorised lines, by teacher or pupils.

Secondly, the teacher also reported that her conversational decision-making was influenced by her prior perceptions of pupils' ability and selfconfidence. Variation in her own behaviour between different administrations of a single conversation were to be accounted for partly in this way: she would be 'more ambitious' with pupils who she knew 'could cope', venturing beyond the known language resource in her own speech and providing less hackneyed responses to pupil initiatives.

TEACHER-PUPIL COOPERATIVE PERFORMANCE

Simple inspection of the conversations would not have revealed this underlying pedagogic dimension to decision-making, as in the main Teacher B was successful in bringing about natural-looking conversations. She sustained her various roles with only occasional lapses (e.g. not knowing what her name was supposed to be, when asked). She consistently took most of the conversational initiatives, but was usually responsive to any taken by the pupils. She avoided teacher-style evaluation of pupil utterances almost completely, except at the end of any given conversation, and usually responded in 'friendly native speaker' style to malformed pupil utterances (ignoring most errors of form, and cooperating in the 'repair' of unintelligible ones). She coped in similar style with pupil non-comprehension, when appropriately signalled:

TB   *Alors, qu'est-ce que tu veux boire, avec ton bifteck?*

PE   *Emm... pommes de terre*

TB   *Qu'est-ce que tu veux boire? Pas manger, boire. Avec ton bifteck - du vin, de l'eau minérale, qu'est-ce que tu veux boire?*

P   *Oh, emm... je ne comprends - je ne comprends pas*

TB   *Tu ne comprends pas? Alors tu veux boire quelquechose, avec ton bifteck? Tu veux boire un verre de vin, ou... em... de l'eau minérale, ou... je ne sais pas, du thé, ou...*

P   *Ahh, emm, du thé*

TB   *Du thé! Bien alors, okay. Mais en France généralement, on ne boit pas de thé avec le bifteck* (etc) ('A table', teacher-pupil pair 3)

Given so much teacher input, no conversation could break down completely. But the majority of the pupils' contributions to these conversations were consequently responses to teacher initiation. Pupils behaviour was contextually aberrant rather more frequently than that of the teacher (e.g. an attempt to bargain over the price of a 'carnet', or a persistent attempt to buy vegetables at a fish stall), but was in the main consistent with their role. They were only occasionally able to develop topical links between successive question/answer exchanges in the more open, social conversations however, and were often either unable or unwilling to employ any 'repair' strategies (such as saying *Je ne comprends pas*), instead commonly stopping dead and waiting to be rescued when communication broke down! (However, the teacher felt this was partly a byproduct of the testing framework).

SIMULATIONS: INTRODUCTION

The two simulation studies carried out during the action research phase had many resemblances with the role play activities reported in foregoing sections of this chapter. However, the demands these tasks made on pupils' communicative FL competence were considered to be more rigorous, in two main ways:

a) Participants were expected to join in the imaginary activity as themselves, and not as some invented character. (Speaking as oneself seemed likely to add to the complexity of the communicative tasks, since potentially at least, the pupils' FL competence might be called on to express their own individual experiences, feelings and preferences, rather than the few stock behaviours likely to be associated with a role such as 'waiter' or 'market stall holder'.)

b) The tasks were constructed so that successful completion depended on a more sustained process of information-sharing and negotiation between participants than was required in the role play tasks.

The two simulation studies were both conducted at S2 level. The activities were broadly similar: in each case pairs of pupils tried to arrange a joint outing. Each participant was equipped with previously prepared diary information, individualised and unknown to his/her partner; the task was meant to involve the exchange of this diary information, and negotiation of the joint outing taking the diary material into account.

Simulation 1

SUMMARY DESCRIPTION

The first simulation study was conducted at Sweet Grammar School, in term 3 of the school year. Teacher J carried out the same activity with two mixed-ability S2 classes. In a previous lesson each class had prepared a written diary of the week in their jotters, including a mixture of real and invented plans for activities, outings, etc. In the simulation activity itself the pupils were supposed to arrange joint outings over the telephone, in pairs or threes, taking account of this diary information.

The activity was explained and managed through French. In each case, one impromptu model of the activity was also given before the pupils attempted it. On the first occasion the model was provided by the teacher and the French assistant, who was present throughout the lesson. On the second occasion the teacher modelled the conversation with a pupil.

27 members of class A were present for the experiment, 25 members of class B. The pupils worked in pairs/groups for about ten minutes on the first occasion, about sixteen minutes on the second. Meanwhile the teacher (and assistant, with class A) circulated and involved himself in the individual conversations of the pupils, and the researcher recorded as many conversations as possible. When he judged the pupils to have had sufficient time, the teacher reverted to a whole-class discussion, ending the lesson by questioning individual pairs about their joint decisions.

During later lessons pupils were withdrawn (in their working pairs/threes), and interviewed by the researcher about their understanding of the activity and their performance of it.

TEACHER COMMENTS

In post-mortem discussion, Teacher J argued strongly for regular inclusion of activities of this type in pupils' learning programmes; he saw them as motivating and useful in preparing pupils to handle specific sorts of situations and kinds of talk, as well as providing opportunities for re-using and applying new language material. Comparing the two attempts at the activity, the teacher said he preferred the version in which two fluent speakers provided the initial model conversation. This facilitated the demonstration of the conversational possibilities of the pupils' existing language resource, as well as challenging them by the inclusion of unfamiliar elements; it also facilitated the inclusion of humour. The teacher accepted that a too-fluent model might be alienating for pupils (though he did not feel this had been a problem on this occasion); a teacher-pupil model might be easier for pupils to identify with, and might also reveal unexpected problem areas in the pupils' language resource, which could be sorted out before the whole class tackled the activity. However, he argued the fully fluent model was, in the long term, more beneficial.

PUPIL PERFORMANCE

The fourteen recorded pairs/groups of pupils produced conversations between one and seven transcript pages in length. Unsurprisingly those conversations in which the teacher became involved tended to be longer than others. The conversations also differed in the amount of 'depth' with which possible options for joint outings were discussed. Generally speaking the pupils with least to say about each date they discussed were those who (from interview evidence) understood the task in the simplest sense, that of merely 'matching' diary information (see next section). Those who interpreted the task as involving persuasion tended to produce the largest numbers of speech turns.

However, success in arranging joint outings, and conversational length, were not the only possible criteria in judging the quality of the recorded conversations. These also varied considerably in the degree of explicitness, and level of detail, with which certain key conversational functions were performed, and in the extent to which certain types of argument were sustained.

COMPARISON WITH TA CONVERSATION

The model conversation recorded by Teacher J and the FL assistant (the TA conversation) is used as a reference point in the detailed discussion of pupil performance which follows. This conversation began with the briefest identification and greetings exchanges possible, consonant with the supposed 'telephone call' context. The rest of the conversation was organised around the consideration of possible activities on successive days of the week. Here is the full discussion about one day, Thursday:

TJ	*Eh bien, que fais-tu jeudi?*
A	*Ahh, jeudi - ahh jeudi, c'est moi... qui va voir un film*
TJ	*Ah, tu vas au cinéma*
A	*Oui, on joue un film comique*
TJ	*Ah, un film comique. De - de qui?*
A	*Ah, c'est un vieux film comique, avec Charlot*
TJ	*Avec -*
A	*Charlot. Tu connais?*
TJ	*Ahh, c'est un film - un film français*
A	*Non, un film américain, avec... Charlot, c'est Charlie Chaplin*

TJ   *Ahh, bien sûr. Ah non, je n'aime pas ça. Moi je préfère Laurel and Hardy, ou bien Tom et Jerry*

A   *Ah bon*

TJ   *Mais écoute, écoute -*

A   *Qu'est'ce que tu fais jeudi?*

TJ   *Jeudi je vais à la disco. Alors toi, tu ne veux pas aller à la disco jeudi?*

A   *Non, je vais à la disco mercredi*

TJ   *Ah oui, mais... ça ne fait rien*

A   *Hmm non, j'ai acheté les bill; les tickets de cinéma*

TJ   *Ah. Bon, alors, il y a le vendredi* (etc)

Here is a similar section from a pupil conversation:

P1   Excuse me, is it (the tape recorder) on? Is it on? Oh well, right. *Ehh, bonjour*

P2   *Bonjour*

P1   *Ça va?*

P2   *Oui, ça va bien, merci*

P1   *Emm, où vas-tu à lundi?*

P2   *Lundi une ehh...*
      (Whispering)

P1   *Ahh, je vais aller à un concert! Ehh, quelle sorte concert?*

P2   *Ehh, un* new - new *romantique*

P1   *Ahh, moi j'aime (...). Emm, que - quel groupe (...)?*

P2   *Emm, Duran Duran*

P1   *Ah, oui! Moi, à lundi, je... je vais aller à - maison des jeunes...*

P2   *Quelle heure est-il?*

P1   (whispers) *A quelle heure?*

P2   *A quelle heure?*

P1   *Emm... est à six heures. Est à Dxxxx. Tu aimes - tu aimes le pingpong? Tu aimes le pingpong?*

P2   *Non*

P1   *Ahh?*

P2   *Non, c'est... ennuyant*

P1   *Ohh, moi j'aime le pingpong. Ehh, qu'est-ce que tu vas faire, ehh le concert a fini?*

P2   *Ehh, le restaurant?*

P1   *Ahh, le restaurant! Ehh - Chi - Chinese?*

P2   *Oui*

P1   *Ah oui, ehh c'est cher?*

P2   *Oui, c'est cher*

P1   *(...) ... tu aimes le Chinese?*
P2   *(...)*
P1   *Moi-ah, oui, oui, oui. Je préfère le...Indian*
P2   *Non, non, (...)*
P1   *Emm, où vas-tu ehh - à mardi?* (A1)

As appears from these examples, the main conversational elements in both TA and pupil conversations were queries and statements about plans and intentions, together with evaluative comments and reactions about these plans, positive and negative. Explicit invitations to join in an activity were unexpectedly rare (only three examples in the TA conversation); it seems that most of the time, a statement of intention to do something was 'understood' as an invitation to the other to join in, while a negative evaluative comment, or an alternative statement of intention, were 'understood' as a refusal.

RANGE OF EXPONENTS

Teacher and assistant used a resonable variety of exponents to perform the commonest functions of inquiring into and stating intentions, and evaluating them. Commonly used forms for queries and statements about **intentions** were utterances of the form:

(Time Phrase) + *je vais* + VP (avec N)   (11 instances)
(Time P) + *je vais* + Prep P   (avec N) (6)
(Time P) + *je veux* + VP   (3)
(Time P) + *tu vas* + Prep P   (3)
Que fais-tu/Qu'est-ce que tu fais (+ Time P)   (5).

The teacher and assistant thus showed a clear tendency to 'speak in sentences' in realising these types of move. Altogether they produced only nine exponents for such informing moves which consisted of a Time, Prepositional or Verb Phrase only.

In contrast, most pupils produced a substantially higher proportion of sub-sentential exponents for these 'informing' moves, such as Time, Prepositional or Noun Phrases. However, most also produced exponents of the type:

(Time P) + *je vais* + VP.

Indeed, this was the commonest single structure used in the entire corpus, and the minority of pupil pairs or individuals who failed to use it seemed obliged to fill the gap with some equivalent though non-standard exponent:

A *mardi je jouer au golf* (B1)

Moi est... visiter ma ehh camarade à la surprise partie (A4)

The **attitudinal/evaluative** comments found in the TA model conversation were brief, and mostly fell into a fairly small number of structural categories:

Je/tu n'aime(s) pas + NP (4)

Je préfère + NP (2)

(C'est) + Adj/Adv (9)

Ce n'est pas + Adj (2)

· *Il (n) y a (pas)* + NP (5)
(e.g. *il n'y a pas de bons programmes*)

Of the fourteen recorded pupil conversations, eight included a range of three or more forms to express evaluative comments (other than *oui/non* plus appropriate tones of voice!), the remainder having two or fewer. In the pupil data *aimer* figured prominently, with or without negation; the commonest adjectives found (almost always either alone or in the structure *c'est* + Adj. were: *bon, drole, ennuyeux, cher, interessant, excellent.* There were a few less successful attempts to go beyond the range of structures found in the TA model:

P1   *Ehh jeudi il y a ....* nothing *.... on télé*
P2   *On télé?*
P1   *Oui. Il y a .... non. Il est ennuyeux on jeudi* (B6)

We have already noted that, in their model conversation, the teacher and assistant issued explicit **invitations** in relation to only some of the dates about which they were negotiating. The three invitations they did produce all took the form:

Tu (ne) veux (pas) aller + Prep P (+ Time P) *(avec moi)*
(e.g. *Tu ne veux pas aller a la disco jeudi?*)

Of the recorded pupil conversations, a minority included no explicit invitations at all, but used statements of plans and evaluative comments, perhaps supplemented by *oui* or *non* for the 'inviting' function (and for 'refusing' as in the following example):

P1   <u>*Vendredi je visiter à la patinoire à Glasgow. C'est drôle...Oui?*</u>
P2   *Hmm?*
P1   *Oui?*
P2   *Oh -*
P1   *A vendredi*
P2   *(........)*
P1   *Je visiter à la patinoire, c'est drôle*
P2   <u>*Non, au disco.*</u> (B1)

In a couple of cases, pupils made it clear that they felt an explicit invitation was appropriate, but could not find a form to express one:

P1   ...How do you ask emm - how do you ask ... if you want to come with us?
P2   *Eh?*
P1   How do you say that? (B1)

One pupil modelled for her partner:

P2   *Mardi ehh.... ehh à discothèque.*
           Oh no, *aux courses*
           (....)
P1   *Moi, j'aime les - moi j'aime les - moi, j'aime les courses!* Ask me to come with you.
P2   *Oui, emm....*
P1   (models) <u>*Tu vas aux courses -*</u>
P2   *Tu vas aux courses -*
P1   (models) <u>*Avec moi?*</u>
P2   *Avec moi?*
P1   *Ahh merci, (....) bien, oui* (A1)

Some pupils resorted to self-invitation:

P2   *Queens Hall?*
P1   *Oui, c'est bon*
P2   <u>*C'est possible à ... moi?*</u>
P1   *Oui*
P2   <u>*Moi?*</u> *A quelle heure?* (B9)

Altogether only three recorded conversations included invitations of the form modelled by the teacher and assistant:

P1   *Ehh, on ... on samedi, <u>tu veux jouer au football avec moi?</u>*
P2   *Oui ...*
P1   *Ah oui, emm ... Ehh à la Black Park, à dix heures?* (B4)

While the linkage between particular language functions and their exponents is never a simple matter, nonetheless as we have seen it was possible to pick out certain form function correspondences in this data as far as certain key task components were concerned, namely **stating intentions, evaluating** them and **issuing invitations.** No such correspondences could be identified for the last major function the pupils were expected to perform: that of **persuading** their partners to agree to a joint activity. A very varied range of utterance types might be produced in the attempt to persuade, including all those discussed so far. Thus in the interests of persuasion, in the model TA conversation, both participants at different moments expanded on, or requested, details about proposed events, made evaluative comments, and/or tried to elicit the attitudinal positions of their interlocutor:

TJ   *Lundi je vais aller au cinéma. Tu veux aller au cinéma avec moi?*
A   *Oh non, (...). Lundi je vais à une surprise-partie*
TJ   *A une surprise-partie?*
A   *Oui*
TJ   *Mais <u>il y a un très bon western au cinéma</u>*
A   *Mais moi, je vais à une surprise-partie avec mes copains et mes copines*
TJ   *<u>Tu n'aimes pas les westerns?</u>*
A   *Si, mais je préfère la surprise-partie*
TJ   *Ecoute, <u>à quelle heure est-ce que la surprise-partie commence?</u>*
A   *Ehh, la surprise-partie commence à ...huit heures*
TJ   *A huit heures, ohh* (etc)

Such elaborate and lengthy attempts at persuasion were rare in the pupil data, but not unknown:

P1   *En lundi, je vais aller à Glasgow...Je vais prendre le bateau et le train*
P2   *Ohh, oui*

P1	*Tu voudrais aller au Glasgow avec moi? ... Tu voudrais -*
P2	*Non*
P1	*Non? ... Tu es sûr? Oui?...*
P2	*Non*
P1	*Qu'est-ce que tu vas faire?*
P2	*(...)*
P1	*Tu vais aller à la pêche?*
P2	*Oui*
P1	*Mais... tu vais aller à la pêche en dimanche*
P2	*Oui*
P1	*Tu aimes aller à la pêche ...*
P2	*Oui...*
P1	*C'est ennuyeux, aller à la pêche. Je n'aime pas ça*
P2	*Tu aller à la pêche?*
P1	*Emm, oui et non....*
P2	*Ahh, (....)....*
P1	*Emm, tu voudrais aller à Glasgow - aller à Glasgow, oui? .... Tu voudrais aller à Glasgow?*
P2	*Non*
P1	*Non? ....Je vais faire du shopping à Glasgow*
P2	*Non*
P1	*Je vais faire du shopping à Glasgow -*
P2	*Oui -*
P1	*Pour les disques (B6)*

Thus it appeared that the pupils were as skilled as the teacher and assistant in conversational strategy. Where they differed from the fluent speakers was in the linguistic resources available to them to realise the conversational moves they wished to make. As we have seen, the pupils resorted to a variety of tactics to eke out their limited French: making a single structure serve to realise a greater range of purposes, greater use of sub-sentential exponents, use of non-standard FL structures, and the occasional use of English. Their speech also of course differed from that of the model conversation on dimensions such as speed of delivery and accuracy at a morphological level: however, a willingness to tackle the task, and resourcefulness in making do with limited language resources, were striking features of these pupils' efforts.

THE PUPIL INTERVIEWS

This study provided the project's most extended opportunity for talk with pupils about their experience of communicative FL teaching. Their comments provide useful insights into the working of this particular activity, as well as into their more general experience of the communicative approach to FL teaching.

As previously stated, a total of sixteen interviews was conducted. The interviews were semi-structured in form. The main points of interest are summarised below.

PUPILS' UNDERSTANDING OF THE TASK

The pupils' descriptions of the task were categorised according to the different component elements they mentioned. Four basic 'rules of the game' were mentioned by at least some pupils, as follows:

Compare diaries - Eleven of the sixteen pairs/groups said the task involved mutual comparison of the information contained in the individual 'diaries'

Identify joint outing - Seven pairs/groups seemed to be arguing that the task essentially involved checking whether by chance their pre-written diaries already contained matching entries:

RM	*What were you supposed to be doing?*
P	*Talking about what each of us were doing during the week*
RM	*Yes*
P	*To see if they matched up*
RM	*Yes, and if they didn't, what were you supposed to do?*
P	*Ehh...nothing!* (interview with pair B8)

Decide on joint outing - Ten pairs/groups described the task as involving positive decision-making:

You were meant to be phoning your friend and deciding what you could both go to (B9)

We were supposed to organise a day - well, we were supposed to go together (A1)

...One of the days, to make a date to go somewhere together (A6)

Persuade each other - Only four pairs mentioned that the task involved persuasion:

You had got to try and persuade your partner to come to a certain place on a certain day (B1)

> *We were trying to persuade each other to do each others' things* (B10)

Lastly, no pupil suggested that the process of negotiation might involve any **modification** to the given diary plans; even for these pupils who saw the task as involving decision-making and persuasion, there seemed to be an assumption that any prior arrangement was sacrosanct, and that consequently negotiation could occur only in respect of times when one or both pupils had a blank in their 'diaries'.

'REALISM' OF TASK

Only two pairs claimed without qualification that the task resembled real life. The rest argued that it diverged in at least some respects from the kind of conversation they would have with a friend. Much the most commonly mentioned differences were the diary-based nature of the task:

> *Well we wouldn't have a list, probably wouldn't have a list for a start* (B6)

and the perceived requirement exhaustively to compare the given diary material:

> *We went through all the days when doing the task, and usually you just say, you know, 'would you come on Monday?' or something like that* (A6)

> *You wouldn't say all the other days, where you were going and that* (B4)

Pupils clearly felt real life negotiations would be more impromptu, immediate, and flexible:

> *You wouldn't be comparing fixed plans. I mean, you'd make up something, and then you'd change it, just whatever you want to do* (A7)

> *I don't suppose you would really need to persuade your friend* (B11)

Unsurprisingly, they commented too that real life conversations would be more fluent:

There'd be lots of wee bits you'd put in, that you don't know in French (B10).

DECISION-MAKING

While the pupils generally agreed that the task diverged in important respects from 'real life', they had nonetheless taken account of reality in deciding what to put in their 'diaries'. Only six pupils claimed the diary information was entirely true, but six pairs and six individuals said it was partly true, partly made up, and eight pairs said the events listed were the sort of things they might do. Nonetheless, only three pupils had specially requested FL phrases appropriate to individual diary activities (babysitting, canoeing); the rest drew from a pool of known phrases.

Pupils did not find it easy to talk in detail about their ongoing conversational decision-making and mostly limited what they said to fairly general comments. A minority suggested they took part in such activities in an unselfconscious, non-reflective way: *We just come out with things like we were talking normal, in English* (A2). The majority, however, suggested an ongoing at least partial concern with language form: *You are thinking what to say, and how you say it in French* (A1). There was an understanding that the 'rules of the game' required talk in quantity; one pupil said he would *say anything like, just trying to keep it going* (B4). But the requirement for producing 'proper conversation' was also recognised. One strategy mentioned for producing enough of the right kind of talk was recall: *At the beginning all you really do is try and remember what you have to say...* (A3). This pupil mentioned another way of maximising fluency: *It is mostly the things you know best that you say. (....) You prefer to avoid words that you are not sure of, and go round them* (ibid). Other strategies for keeping things going are apparent in remarks such as: *I ask him (partner) what to say, and then he tells me* (B7); and *if you don't know a word, you just say it in English* (A6). Pupils were conscious of gaps between conversational aspirations and their realisation: *You're wanting to do it good, but (...) usually when you start doing it, it is all garbled, you know, speaking* (B9).

REACTIONS TO FL-MEDIUM INSTRUCTIONS

The pupils were asked for their reactions to the use of French by the teacher in setting up the activity. They were unanimous that it was

not a problem on this particular occasion. However, half of the pairs
said the teacher's use of French for instruction-giving sometimes
caused difficulties. The most commonly mentioned problem was the
requirement for sustained concentration:

> *Well it takes a while sometimes you know, he demonstrates it
> and - till you get the right idea. Sometimes it can take quite a
> long while to get to know what he is going on about* (A3).

P	*Sometimes when he talks an awful lot, then you just kind of switch off, because he talks that much, and you don't understand it, and you just -*
RM	*You kind of give up*
P	*Don't kind of listen to the rest of it* (B8)

The teacher's commonest tactics for conveying meaning had been
noticed by several pupils:

(REPETITION)
*You don't normally understand the first time, but he normally
says it about ten times to make sure* (B6)

(ESTABLISHING ROUTINES)
*You get used to the words that he says, he always uses the same
words to explain things, and you understand them* (B5)

(PARAPHRASE & USE OF COGNATES)
*You can usually guess though, because he usually puts it in a
couple of different words, and one of the words is like an English
word, and you can usually work out what he is meaning* (B10)

(MIME & GESTURE)
*He usually... describes it with his hands, and gives a book or
something, or ...* (B10)

(PUPIL INTERPRETING)
*He asks the class if you understand, and if you didn't
understand, then you got it said to you in English by one person
out of the class. So it wasn't really that bad* (B9).

Less explicitly, the pupils referred to their own active strategies for comprehension:

> *If you hear something you know (in what) he is saying, try and work out from there* (A6)

P	*Sometimes he says things, and you don't know what he is saying*
RM	*So what do you do then?*
P	*Tell him you don't know what he is saying*
RM	*You are not embarrassed to tell him? (...)*
P	*It is all right* (A6)
	I usually ask somebody else (A7)

TEACHER-ASSISTANT MODELLING

The five pairs from class A, that for which the teacher and FL assistant had modelled the task, were asked how helpful the model had been. Three pairs felt it had been useful: *It gave us an example what you were expected to do* (A6); *Then you know the sort of things that you have to say in it* (A7). But two pairs expressed some alienation from the high-powered model: *You don't really pay attention to things like that, because they don't really seem like what you are going to be doing* (A3).

USEFULNESS OF TASK

Lastly, the pupils were asked to comment on the usefulness of the task. A minority commented instead on the usefulness or otherwise of learning French; of those who commented on paired speaking itself, most did so favourably. Benefits mentioned included the development of vocabulary:

> *Well if we keep doing them, then we will learn, you know, words, because usually he teaches us something new, and then you have got to use it in the conversation* (B5).

and consolidation of existing knowledge:

> *It's usually remembering things that we have been taught* (B1).

But the most commonly mentioned advantage, referred to by a majority of pairs/groups, was the claim that paired speaking was good preparation for future face to face contacts with native speakers:

> *If you were in a conversation with somebody you would have a fair idea of what to say* (A1).

> *It gets you used to having a conversation in French* (B11).

> *You're not just listening to it and writing it down, I think, you're actually trying it out* (B4).

> *You learn to express yourself more* (B6).

A couple of pupils explicitly compared the perceived usefulness of speaking with other activities:

> *I suppose if you write things down you know how to spell them, but if you don't know how to speak them then it is not going to be much use, because you are not going to be writing everything down if you go to France* (B3).

Alongside this general acceptance of the face validity of paired speaking activities, which was challenged only by those who felt French itself was not useful, some comments were made which suggested the classroom reality of doing them was not unalloyed pleasure. Boredom and indiscipline were mentioned as intermittent problems by a few pairs:

> *Sometimes you fall asleep* (A3).

> *Sometimes I don't really want to do it, but most of the times I do it* (B7).

> *Well, I think it is quite good to have to do paired speaking. Occasionally, you know. But the boys behind us, they make lots of noise* (A7).

Several pairs compared talking with a partner favourably with talking to the teacher, however - though one pupil commented in favour of a degree of social distance:

> *If you don't really know them then you'd tend to talk a bit more French than you do if you know the guy you are talking to. Like, a lot of English tends to go into it* (A2).

Simulation 2

SUMMARY DESCRIPTION

The second simulated negotiation study was conducted by Teacher M at Jespersen Academy, with a single upper-set S2 class in the first term of the school year. Twenty-eight pupils were present for the experimental lesson. The pupils were seated in pairs and were issued with pairs of cards prepared by the teacher. Each card was different and contained a week's diary information; the object of the activity was again for pairs of pupils to arrange a joint outing, based on the card material.The pairs of cards were devised so that it was normally possible to arrange an outing without cancelling any prearranged activities.

The activity was introduced and managed through English. After the introduction the teacher modelled the activity twice, with two different pupils. The pupils then did the activity three times in pairs swapping pairs of cards, but not partners, between attempts. After each attempt the pupils were asked to note down which cards they had had, and what arrangement they had made. The entire experiment took approximately 25 minutes; twelve of the fourteen pupil pairs were successfully recorded during at least one attempt at the activity.

TEACHER COMMENTARY

In a preliminary 'post-mortem' discussion, Teacher M and the researcher reviewed transcripts of several recorded conversations. They agreed most pupils had had a clear understanding of what to do and had tackled the task conscientiously. The teacher felt the activity had been worthwhile and enjoyable for the pupils; she said she 'would certainly do it again'. However, she found the pupil conversations diverged from her expectations in certain respects: she had expected them to make a date and then conclude the conversations, for example, whereas several pairs continued until they had exhaustively discussed the card material. As far as the pupils' language performance was concerned, the teacher felt their strategies for 'inviting' were somewhat deficient, and that more preliminary work might have been done to develop their language resources in this area. She reacted differently to the pupils' failure to include comments evaluating plans and proposals however: *Well*

I think it was maybe too complicated for them. In retrospect the teacher again defended her decision to introduce and manage the activity in English; unless exceptionally with a class of high fliers, she felt the activity was too complex to introduce via the target language.

PUPIL PERFORMANCE

The teacher's L1 instructions implied that fairly short, straightforward conversations were expected, and this was confirmed by the two model conversations. The first was as follows:

TM	Okay then, let's just see how the conversation goes
P	*Je vais disco en ville*
TM	What day of the week?
P	*Vendredi*
TM	*Vendredi. Ah non, vendredi je vais à une surprise partie chez Pierre. Ehh, je vais à un concert à Glasgow lundi. Tu viens?*
P	*Ah non, je vais au match de football du stade*
TM	*Ohh, alors! Je vais... à la piscine municipale mercredi. Tu viens?*
P	*Ah oui*
TM	*Ah oui, bon. C'est à trois heures. D'accord? A trois heures, d'accord? ... Okay, d'accord?*
P	Aye
TM	*Alors au revoir, à mercredi. Bon.* Okay, thank you Karen...

After modelling, the phrases *je vais* and *tu viens* were re-modelled at pupil request. However, a pupil who asked for a new language item was directed back to familiar material:

P	How do you say, 'I'm free to go'?
TM	Well, don't - just say what you can say. You don't need to say it all fancy. You might just say *'oui, d'accord'*, okay. That's fine, that's fine, *'d'accord'*, you know how to say *'d'accord'*.

While the desire on the teacher's part to keep things simple seems clear, nonetheless completion of the task as she intended it involved making several types of conversational move, similar to those entailed in Simulation 1: **statements of intention** (again supported by written plans), **evaluative comments**, and **invitations**. (**Persuasion**, however, was apparently not expected.)

The main difference lay in the use of a more restricted set of exponents from these conversational moves.

This setting of limits to linguistic expectations (and indeed the use of English to introduce the task) did not mean that all recorded pairs successfully completed the negotiation task, any more than in Simulation 1. However, out of the fifteen conversations recorded by twelve pupil pairs, ten contained an unambiguous arrangement compatible with the diary cards. (Nobody cancelled or overrode given diary information; most pupils failing to make a clear date compatible with the cards seem to have misheard or misreported card information about day or activity.)

There was considerable variation in the numbers of dates discussed by different pupil pairs, arising from differing interpretations of the requirements of the task. In Simulation 1, virtually all the pupils had discussed the contents of their 'diaries' in full; in Simulation 2, some pairs discussed the diaries exhaustively while others felt under no obligation to do so, and ended the conversation as soon as one arrangement had been made:

P1 *Je - je vais à mardi ... à disco à l'école, je viens?*
P2 *Ehh d'accord, magnifique*

(End of conversation)

As she made clear in interview, the teacher had expected all pupils to adhere to this more limited interpretation of the task; while this was not made explicit in her preliminary instructions to the class, the model conversations used the diary information in a non-exhaustive manner. It seems likely that where pupils went beyond the expected minimum, some very general classroom rules such as 'Speak as much French as possible', 'Don't waste any written information', had not been overridden by the instructions and models for this particular task.

However many dates they talked about, the pupils limited themselves to a small number of speech turns per date. These consisted almost entirely of conversational moves asking about and describing plans, evaluating them, and inviting/accepting/refusing.

Statements about plans in the two model conversations all took the form

Time Phrase + *je vais* + Prepositional Phrase
(e.g. *Vendredi je vais à une surprise-partie chez Pierre*)

In the pupil conversations utterances like this were also common; they were however outnumbered by two other types. The commonest form was the sub-sentential Time P + NP, e.g. *Emm, le jeudi, match de rugby* (2/1), *Samedi.... ehh magasin de discos* (6/2). Next commonest was the non standard *je vais* + NP (+ Time P) e.g. *Je vais un surprise partie à vendredi* (2/1), *Je vais au mercredi le disco au centre* (10/2).

While the form *Je vais* was thus very commonly used, and was completely absent from only two of the fifteen conversations, there is evidence that pupils were not fully confident in using it, in the appearance of a number of forms apparently substituting for it:

A samedi, je.. aller à la peche avec - au Paul... (5/1)

Je - je fais au dîner au restaurant le jeudi, tu viens? (1/3)

However, the frequent use of sub-sentential forms may be interpreted not as reflecting any lack of mastery of *je vais*, but as arising from a desire for variation, conscious or unconscious. The wish to widen the scope of expression may also underlie the pupils' use of a limited number of other more or less non-standard forms, as their ideas perhaps outran their mastery of French:

P1   *(....) Je vais vendredi, samedi, dimanche weekend de ski. Tu vas?*

P2   *Ah non... je vais un surprise-partie à vendredi. Tu vais?*

P1   *Non, <u>est vendredi weekend de ski!</u>* (1/1)

The fact that the pupils, still only in the early stages of S2, had not yet encountered the '*aller* + infinitive' construction was a constraint on the clear expression of some kinds of plans:

P1   <u>*Je vais emm lundi eh promenade en ville*</u>. *Ehh tu vais?*

P2   *Non, pas ça! Emm mardi, promenade de velo*

P1   *Oui! ... Je veux bien.* (1/1)

Altogether, seventeen different standard and non-standard ways of stating/enquiring into plans and intentions could be identified in this group of pupil conversations, with up to six different ways occurring in individual conversations. The other types of move were, however, expressed much more economically by the pupils, if at all. In her second model conversation the teacher had proposed the **evaluation** of plans and intentions, modelling the phrase *J'aime ça* for the purpose. As things turned out this particular phrase was not adopted in any of the recorded conversations. Only seven conversations included any explicit evaluative comments at all. The total FL corpus was:

Non, je n'aime pas + NP (2 occurrences)

Magnifique (2)

Bien (3)

Bon (1).

Thus most usually, the evaluation of proposed plans remained implicit, to be understood from the acceptance/refusal of invitations. These **invitations**, together with **acceptances/refusals**, were themselves frequently not explicitly stated. Again, the teacher had modelled one possible exponent for the 'inviting' function:

Je vais club des jeunes à lundi....d'accord? (9/2)

D'accord featured much more regularly, however, in the business of **accepting** an invitation. The only other exponent of 'acceptance' found (apart from *Oui*) was a solitary *Je veux bien* (1/1). **Refusing** was restricted almost completely to *Non*, apart from a single expansion to *Non, pas ça* (1/1)

In this group of conversations, therefore, exponents with the primary function of providing information about plans and intentions were also regularly expected to do much other conversational 'work', in particular to convey invitations and refusals. However, the conversations were again impressive in the degree of skill displayed by participants in achieving their set conversational purpose with limited FL resources.

CONCLUSION

What general conclusions can be drawn from the experience of the six action research studies reported in this chapter? Firstly, the face validity of the various activities among pupils was a strong contributory factor to high levels of pupil involvement in all role play/simulation activities.

Secondly, the activities were all successful in eliciting from pupils considerable quantities of French, relevant to a variety of situations, embodying a considerable range of functions and of exponents, and with an overall 'communicative' character. These studies therefore support the inclusion of role play and simulation activities in any overall strategy designed to promote classroom learners' communicative FL experience.

There was some variation within the group of six studies; notably, qualitative differences did emerge between the two main types. The simulation studies generally speaking produced conversations with greater discourse coherence, and more sustained topical development, than did the role play tasks. This suggests that activities involving information exchange and negotiation on the basis of pupils' own experience are potentially the more valuable.

However, the effectiveness of these activities in eliciting communicative FL performance from pupils must be attributed at least partly to factors differentiating them from 'real life' interaction. The topics and situations were carefully selected by the teachers in the light of an intimate knowledge of pupils' presumed future 'needs'. The use of introductory impromptu modelling served to remind pupils of the communicative possibilities open to them through exploitation of their existing language resource. In the resulting conversations pupils showed themselves very ready to follow such guidance, and only occasionally allowed their communicative requirements to outrun the linguistic means already to hand. While the resulting conversations met communicative criteria of purpose, unpredictability, discourse coherence, etc, such positive control and restriction of communicative requirements could not be sustained in real life interaction with native speakers.

An important limitation was that all the role play and simulation activities studied for this project were of the 'summative' type, fitted within the 'stages' model of L2 learning; they were carried out at or near the end of a unit of work, and were designed to provide opportunities for re-use of language material already thoroughly familiar from a range of practice FL activities. Given that pupils hardly ventured beyond this familiar ground, these studies produced no interpretable evidence on the usefulness of role play in encountering and assimilating significant amounts of new language material.

CHAPTER 4

ACTION RESEARCH STUDIES II: INFORMATION-ORIENTATED ACTIVITIES

INTRODUCTION

As reported in Chapter 2, during the Stage 2 period of general observation, certain 'biases' were apparent in the types of activity arranged by participating teachers which involved communicative FL use. The most common such activities were both oral and interactive in character, and typically had a primarily **social** or **instrumental** communicative purpose. Only rarely did communicative FL activities have a more **information-orientated** purpose, such as the giving of 'grammar' rules, or imparting background information about French culture. If such information-orientated activities happened at all (and in some classrooms none were observed), they usually happened through English.

This pattern was explored to some extent in interviews which took place during the observational visits. Some teachers argued strongly for the use of English during such episodes, on different grounds:

a) It was important to ensure that all pupils grasped certain information and ideas, and for this it was necessary to use English in talking about them.

b) Episodes in which the French way of life was explained and discussed in a relaxed and informal manner were important both in forming positive attitudes towards French culture and in consolidating the social unity of the mixed ability S1/S2 class as a group. If French were to be used during such episodes, at least some pupils would be placed under extra stress and might experience alienation.

c) A 'discussion' mode was desirable in dealing with topics with a heavy information content, in which pupils could make substantial contributions, questioning and responding to the information presented. Use of French could turn out to be incompatible with commitment to a discussion mode of work.

A counter-case was argued equally strongly by some other participating teachers, who felt communicative FL use for such activities provided invaluable experience in extended listening, developing skills of prediction, gist extraction, guessing, etc. All these arguments require careful consideration. For the purpose of the Communicative Interaction Project, we were interested in investigating both the feasibility of extended information-giving through the medium of French, and any detectable influences in the amount of information transmitted to the pupils, their level of involvement, and the character of any discussion which arose.

During the action research phase of Stage 2 five teachers agreed to undertake studies of teaching activities with a primarily informational purpose, conducted through the medium of French. These activities were of three types normally conducted through English at S1/S2 level: the presentation of 'background' information about the FL culture (three studies), the teaching of a formal 'grammar point' (one study), and a 'skill training' activity (one study). Following sections of this chapter report on these five studies.

Note

The three studies of 'background' episodes involved the use of French for extended information-giving. In all three, background material about France and/or the French way of life was presented by the teacher as a whole-class oral activity, supported by the showing of slides or filmstrip. Two studies took place at S1 level, and one at S2. The S2 study, and one S1 study, each involved two parallel classes being taught by the same teacher. In every case, the 'experimental' episode took up all or part of a single lesson. The researcher observed and recorded these lessons and took notes on visual aids used and other contextual information. Full transcripts of the lessons were later produced for detailed analysis. On each occasion, immediately following the teaching episode, the pupils were asked to fill in a simple questionnaire to provide details of their recall of information presented by the teacher. (In constructing these questionnaires an attempt was made to check on pupils' grasp of information presented verbally rather than visually, and to avoid information presumed to be already familiar from earlier coursebook material.) The studies also involved discussions with the teachers similar to those reported in Chapter 3 for the role play studies.

ACTION RESEARCH STUDIES

Background 1

SUMMARY DESCRIPTION

The first 'background' study was conducted by Teacher A at Palmer High School. She was responsible for two mixed ability S1 classes and agreed to involve both in the study. The activity devised was a presentation of tourist Paris and involved showing a series of twenty slides.

The fact that Teacher A had two mixed ability first year classes, which she perceived as fairly similar in character, provided an opportunity to make a direct comparison between the treatment of this kind of topic in English and in French. The teacher agreed to tackle the activity in English with one class, and in French with the other. She did so in two successive periods on the same day.

The English version of the activity was tried first using all twenty slides. 29 pupils were present; the transcript of the activity runs to eight pages. (While the teacher stuck to English during the main 'background' activity, organisational preliminaries to this lesson took place in French, as was usual for all this teacher's lessons, and she commented afterwards that she had *really felt very awkward speaking in English. I felt there were so many things I could say in French there, and it was silly to say them in English somehow.* She did also comment, however, that she had at times been consciously limiting what she said in English to this class, to what she knew she could manage later in French.)

The French version of this activity followed immediately, with the second class. Again 29 pupils were present; and eighteen slides were shown. The transcript of the French version runs to eleven pages, during which the teacher spoke two words of English (confirming a pupil guess at meaning).

PUPIL QUESTIONNAIRE

Immediately after the activity, each class was given a brief questionnaire to check on their comprehension and short term recall of some of the basic factual information covered in the teacher's presentation.

On the evidence of the questionnaire, the pupils in each class retained fairly similar amounts of the information provided, though the use of English appears to have been more effective for the conveyance of facts at certain moments.

COMPARISON OF ENGLISH AND FRENCH VERSIONS

In each case Teacher A completed the activity as planned, conveying the same or similar information while sticking consistently to the chosen language. Pupils' attention flagged somewhat at times in both lessons; this seemed attributable to the rather long time spent on the activity on both occasions. The following extracts are representative of the general character of the English and French versions of the activity:

(FRENCH PRESENTATION)

TA	*Silence! Ecoutez.* (SLIDE 16) *Alors là, qu'est-ce que c'est?*
P	*La Tour Eiffel*
TA	*La Tour Eiffel, alors la Tour Eiffel, ça mesure 200 mètres, 300 mètres, 400 mètres? Combien de mètres? ... 100, 200, 300, 400? ... Combien?*
P	*Trois -*
TA	*Oui, c'est ça. Trois cents*
P	*Trois cents*
TA	*Trois cents, Oui, ça mesure 300 mètres, alors c'est haut, la Tour Eiffel.*
P	It's high
P	Miss, you can see the lift, half way up (....)
TA	*Où - l'ascenseur, où?*
P	Up at the top bit!
TA	*C'est l'ascenseur là? Je ne sais pas*
P	It's a lift!
TA	*C'est possible, non? Un, deux - ça c'est la troisième étage. L'ascenseur, je ne sais pas où c'est...*
P	Miss, is it - there's grass and parks round it?
TA	*Oui, on va voir. Attends.* (SLIDE 17) *Alors sous l'Arc de Triomphe* (sic) *- Alors il y a une espèce de jardin là, ... Là, vous voyez, ça c'est l'entrée, là. Il y a l'ascenseur, et là il y a l'escalier. Tout le monde comprend 'l'escalier'? Il y a un ascenseur, il y a aussi un escalier*

P   An escalator!

TA   *Non, un escalier, si tu montes à pied*

P   Escalator!

P   Stairs!

TA   *Oui, c'est ça bon. Alors là, l'autre côté, ce bâtiment, ça s'appelle le palais de Maillot* (sic)*, là...*(SLIDE 18) *Voilà. Le palais de Maillot* (etc)

        CHAILLOT

(ENGLISH PRESENTATION)

TA   *(...) Okay? ...* (SLIDE 16) *Right, this you will all recognise. What is it called?*

PP   *The Eiffel Tower! The* Tour Eiffel*!*

TA   *Right, the Eiffel Tower ... Christian, can you remember how high it was in metres?*

P   *A hundred metres*

TA   *No, it's more than that*

P   *Miss! Three hundred and ten!*

TA   *Now, it's about three hundred metres high, so it is very high ... You can either go up by lift, or there are also stairs for the first few stages, you can go up the stairs as well, which is obviously a bit cheaper. And you've a restaurant that we spoke about last time, and shops etc ...*

P   *Miss, can you only walk up so far?*

TA   *Yes, you can only walk up so far ...*

P   *Miss, do you get anoxic on that?*

TA   *No, it is hardly that high ... Have you got a question to ask at the back? You should only be speaking if your hand is up and I've asked you to speak! ... (...) Oh, sorry you're on -* (SLIDE 17) *Right, underneath the Eiffel Tower this time. Gives you an idea of the size of it there. That's just the feet of the thing. But again, you could maybe get a better idea of the stairs - no, you can't really make it out all that well. The lift goes up the tracks on one side, the stairs in the other leg. I can't quite make out which is which there. Though the other side you've got a place called le palais de Chaillot, which we'll see in the next one as well.*

P   *Miss, can you walk up it for nothing?*

TA   *Yes, I don't think you pay to walk up it, if I remember right.*

P   *What's the lift charge?*

TA   *It's fairly expensive in the lift. I think it was about 70 francs - I think it is about 35 francs a person.*

P   *Miss, is that to get to the middle, and up to the top?*

TA   *No, it takes you up to the top and back down again.*
P   *Miss, there's different charges for which one you go to.*
TA   *Yes, it depends how far you go up. See there's different
       stages, so it depends how far you go...*
       Bon, vas-y. (SLIDE 18) *Right, the same place we were looking
       at from the Eiffel Tower a minute ago. There is this* palais de
       M - de Chaillot *(etc)*

In both lessons, as the transcripts show, the teacher was the
predominant speaker. In both, she most frequently introduced each
new slide herself, by telling the children what it showed. For a
minority of the slides, she varied this pattern by asking pupils
questions about what they were looking at, mostly raising points to
do with factual recall, e.g. *What is the river called?* (English
version), *Comment s'appelle la rivière?* (French version).

The absolute number of pupil contributions to the discourse
was also not dissimilar in the two versions of the activity (62 in the
L1 version, 81 in the FL version). In both cases most pupil
utterances were in English.

The quality of the interaction between teacher and pupils did
vary somewhat, however. In the FL version the predominant type
of teacher question to pupils was the 'comprehension check',
explicitly seeking confirmation that the children were following
the French (*Tout le monde comprend?*). A high proportion of the
children's utterances in this version correspondingly consisted in
guesses at the meaning of things the teacher had said, and
indications that they had/had not understood. In the English
version on the other hand such checks were obviously unnecessary.

(FRENCH VERSION)

TA   *Alors ça s'appelle la Con - Concièrgerie*
P   *(...)*
TA   *C'était une prison*
P   A prison!
TA   *Bon, c'était une prison, oui. Non, attendez, pas maintenant!
       C'était une prison*
P   *(...)*
TA   *C'est comme pour Marie-Antoinette et cetéra, c'était une
       prison*
P   *(...)*
TA   *Oui, comme la Bastille*
P   She got her head cut off

TA   *Continue - quoi?*

P   *(...)*

TA   *Mais écoutez! Ce n'est pas une prison maintenant*

P   It's not a prison -

TA   *Pas maintenant*

P   Not now

TA   Not now. *C'était une prison. Bon...*

(ENGLISH VERSION)

TA   *(...) Now that obviously isn't Notre Dame, because it is quite a big island. That is a place called* la Concièrgerie. *Now it used to be a prison. It is not actually used as a prison nowadays - I'm not quite sure what they use it as, but it used to be a prison ... Okay? ...*

It seemed that pupils' and teachers' inevitable concern in the FL version with ensuring comprehension may to some extent have squeezed out other sorts of pupil comments and contributions from the episode.

Lastly, the study provided rich comparative material for a more narrowly linguistic study of FL use by the teacher. The treatment of similar topics in the two languages provided detailed evidence about how FL-using teachers simplify their language to make it more accessible to their pupils. These 'simplification strategies' are considered further in Chapter 7.

Background 2

SUMMARY DESCRIPTION

The second 'background' study was conducted by Teacher E at Bloomfield High School. This study also involved the showing of photos of Paris to an S1 class, this time in the form of filmstrip frames. This class was about to begin the *Tour de France* unit *Le beau Paris*, and the teacher used the background filmstrip provided for the unit, substituting his own FL commentary for the English commentary supplied on tape with the *Tour de France* materials.

25 pupils were present at the lesson which included this activity. The teacher himself worked the filmstrip projector from the rear of the class. Immediately following the activity, a

questionnaire was administered to the pupils to check on the comprehension and recall of factual material presented during the 'background' presentation.

COMMENTARY ON IMPLEMENTATION

Teacher E covered in his commentary all the information given in the pre-packaged English version, including some historical as well as descriptive material, together with a small amount of 'extra' content. He succeeded in presenting this material largely in French (though using some English to help solve some comprehension difficulties). He delivered it much in the style of a taped commentary, presenting the first few filmstrip frames without any encouragement to pupils to comment or to ask questions. Later in the activity he moved towards a somewhat more interactive style, but most questions to pupils consisted in comprehension checks, and the vast majority of pupil utterances consisted of guesses at meaning.

The following extract shows the general character of the presentation:

TE   *(...) Et c'est un monument très célèbre, l'Arc de Triomphe. C'est un monument très célèbre au milieu de Paris, près de l'avenue des Champs-Elysées ...* (SLIDE 4) *Au-dessous de l'Arc de Triomphe nous avons ici la tombe, la tombe du soldat inconnu, pour représenter tous les soldats qui sont morts pendant la première guerre mondiale. Qu'est-ce que c'est, une tombe, une tombe? Oui, Stuart?*

P   (...)

TE   *Oui, est la tombe du soldat inconnu? Oui? ... La tombe du soldat inconnu, oui?*

P   The unknown soldier

TE   The tomb of the unknown soldier, *bon, très bien. Et ça c'est pour représenter tous les soldats, tous les soldats qui sont morts - qui sont morts? Tous les soldats qui sont morts... Hmm? ... Qui sont morts -*

P   (...)

TE   Died, right. *Pendant la première guerre mondiale. Pendant la première guerre mondiale ...La première guerre. Une guerre, c'est -* (Mimes shooting) *Oui?*

P   (...)

TE   What kind of soldiers though?

P	A general?
TE	*Emm, pendant la première guerre mondiale.* During - *la première guerre mondiale*
P	The first world war
TE	*C'est ça,* the first world war. *(...) Alors voici - voici la tombe du soldat inconnu, et ça c'est pour représenter tous les soldats qui sont morts pendant la première, la première guerre mondiale. Tu comprends, Deborah? Non? Tous les soldats - les soldats? Qui sont morts pendant la première guerre mondiale. La guerre,* the war. *Ça va? La première guerre mondiale, qu'est-ce que c'est?*
P	*(...)*
TE	*Première,* first
P	The first soldier?
TE	*Non, non, non.* The first what?
P	World war
TE	First world war, *bon. Très bien* (etc)

As appears from this extract, the teacher's French became linguistically quite complex at certain moments during this activity. The presentation of historical information in particular seemed linked to the use of items such as combinations of past tense forms, relative clauses, and prepositional phrases. Such rich combinations are highly unusual in all the material collected in S1/S2 level for the research project. This may have been partly due to the relatively abstract and decontextualised nature of the historical topic being presented. It may also be partly due to the physical organisation of the activity (teacher at the back, working the filmstrip projector). This meant that the teacher had no eye contact with his audience and was consequently receiving only reduced feedback on the state of pupil comprehension from moment to moment.

The pupil questionnaire data suggested pupil comprehension was uneven. The teacher himself commented that he had been unsure about ongoing levels of comprehension among pupils; he said he had found the process of simplification difficult on this occasion. Teacher E was known from observation at other times to have a highly interactive and responsive style of teaching, and to be both very sensitive to any hint of non-comprehension, and flexible and inventive in solving comprehension difficulties by diverse linguistic and non-linguistic means. His shift on this occasion to a more didactic, less interactive style, and the related uncertainty concerning pupil comprehension levels, may be related to the choice of topic and perhaps also to the lack of direct eye contact between teacher and pupils. This study served to emphasise the importance of both these factors in providing 'comprehensible input' for learners whose FL competence was still at an embryonic stage.

Background 3

The third background study was taught by Teacher J at Sweet Grammar School. It again involved the showing of slides, this time to a mixed ability second-year class of 21 pupils in their third term. The teacher showed a set of twelve slides to do with the cinema and other forms of commercial entertainment (TV, radio, magazines, etc). He spent c.40 minutes on the activity, devoting most time to the first few slides (sixteen minutes for slide 1, seven minutes for slide 2).

PUPIL QUESTIONNAIRE

At the conclusion of the activity, as a check on pupils' understanding and retention of the material presented, the pupils were again asked to provide written answers to certain questions in English. In this case they were asked more 'open' questions, being invited to list as many points of information as they could remember relating to slides 1 and 2 (which were re-projected as prompts to memory).

All pupils but one remembered at least one 'fact' relating to slide 1, and most listed at least three, with twelve pupils listing five or more. However, though the teacher had spent some time trying to explain the French film certification system, most of the fifteen pupils who mentioned this gave inaccurate information. All but two pupils remembered something of slide 2, with most listing two, three or four accurate items of information.

COMMENTARY

In this activity the slides provided only a starting point for the discussion. Thus, for example, the first two slides showing the exterior of a cinema, and some posters, triggered a wide-ranging presentation about the French cinema, including information about the invention of the cinema by Louis Lumière, about the film certification system and about the use of dubbing. Teacher J adopted an interactive style of presentation in this activity, typically introducing new topics with questions intended to involve pupils in identifying and developing them (e.g. *Qui est-ce qui a inventé le téléphone/la radio/le cinéma? Voilà des magazines, quelles sortes de magazines?*).

The pupils made a substantial contribution to the discourse; just over 200 pupil utterances can be counted in the transcript. These were mostly in English, however, and a relatively small number of pupils contributed a high proportion of the total. Most of these pupil utterances were either responses to 'substantive' questions of the type just exemplified, or else to do with the negotiation of comprehension - guesses at meaning, etc. About a dozen pupil utterances took the form of unprompted questions and comments about the topics of discussion (e.g. *How do they understand our records?*).

The following extract comes from the discussion arising from a slide showing two French cinema posters. Both were for American films:

TJ   *Bien, imaginez - imaginez que vous êtes en France. Au cinéma, il y aura toujours beaucoup de films américains dans les cinémas*

P   There's a lot of American films

TJ   *Oui. Il y a beaucoup de films américains dans les cinémas. Pourquoi?*

P   Because they don't make very many of their own?

TJ   *Mm. En France, le cinéma est une industrie... importante*

P   An important industry

TJ   *Ehh... on fait, on tourne de très bons films en France. (...) Le - le cinéma français est très bon... mais naturellement ce sont les Américains qui tournent beaucoup de films populaires. N'est-ce pas? Des films avec ehh Robert Redford et Paul Newman et James Cann et Burt Reynolds et - et cetera. Ce sont des films très populaires, et naturellement... naturellement on peut voir ces films en France, dans les cinémas français. Mais - voici une question. Imaginez que vous êtes français, hein? Et vous allez au cinéma pour voir un film de - de James Cann, par exemple. ... Vous aimez James Cann, il est très bon vedette de cinéma, et vous allez voir un de ses films. ... Qu'est-ce que vous allez écouter? Naturellement vous voyez James Cann, mais qu'est-ce que vous écoutez? ...*

P	*In anglais*
TJ	*Hmm?*
P	Its in English if they don't change it.
TJ	*C'est en anglais?*
P	They change it to French!
TJ	*Voilà la question. C'est en anglais?*
P	They get other actors to act - to mime it (...)
TJ	*Oui, c'est ça. Les films - des films comme ça, sont doublés.*
P	Dubbed
TJ	Dubbed, *c'est ça. Les films sont doublés en français. Alors il y a des - des acteurs français ...qui parlent. Alors vous allez voir un film de James Cann, ce n'est pas James Cann qui parle. C'est un acteur français.*
PP	A French actor
TJ	*Et tous - tous ces films, ces films populaires, sont doublés...*
P	Dubbed
TJ	*Oui... Bon...* (etc)

(goes on to explain that subtitling is not popular in France)

This extract shows Teacher J attempting to convey relatively decontextualised and abstract information comparable to that attempted in Background 1. This attempt appeared considerably more successful, partly because of the greater FL competence which S2 pupils may be assumed to possess, but also partly because of a more extensive and flexible use of simplification strategies by the teacher.

TEACHER COMMENTS

Unlike the teachers involved in Background 1 and 2, Teacher J did not see the presentation of background material via French as an 'innovation'. He said he routinely presented such material via French when the material itself was suitable (as he judged this 'cinema' material to be, due to its close parallels with the British situation), and with pupils who were sufficiently advanced. (*You can't tackle this sort of thing in Unit 1.*)

On this occasion he said he had completed the activity much as planned, sticking to French in his own speech except for very occasional one or two-word English phrases, confirming pupil guesses at meaning. It took slightly longer than intended, but the teacher argued that the time taken, and disproportionate time spent on the different slides, had been appropriate. Not all pupils were equally involved, but Teacher J felt this would have been the case whichever language had been used. In fact, he argued that levels of involvement were perhaps slightly higher than they would have been in English, given the extra concentration required for comprehension. It was hard to gauge levels of comprehension among pupils who said little - but even in English, such pupils' involvement was problematic. The teacher felt the extent of pupil comments had not been significantly reduced by the use of French.

Teacher J commented that he had sometimes run out of possibilities in trying to solve comprehension difficulties via French! This had been the case in the attempt to explain the film certification system, where after several attempts he had 'cut his losses' and moved on to a new topic, although aware that many pupils had failed to grasp the details of the system. 'Failures' such as this were to be regularly expected, the teacher felt, in using the foreign language for this type of activity. He was not put off by it, and was generally happy with the levels of comprehension achieved. In fact, he commented in conclusion that if repeating the activity, he would behave very similarly. His view that the topic was suitable for presentation through French, because of its relative familiarity as well as the existence of many cognate words in the relevant vocabulary, had been borne out.

Grammar study

INTRODUCTION

During the observation phase of Stage 2 it was noticeable that any extended discussion which took place **about** the French language was conducted in English. The teachers observed at this stage appeared to vary considerably in the extent to which they felt that the giving of rules, or the discussion of concepts such as 'gender', were appropriate at S1/S2 level. Some regularly included episodes of this type in their lessons, while others hardly ever did so, holding instead to an 'inductive' approach which relied almost entirely on practice and example. The teachers who spoke most French were among this latter group. It was not clear whether they felt talking about grammar was in any case unnecessary for S1/S2, or whether they felt it was incompatible with keeping up an all-French commitment. But for whatever reason, it turned out that 'talking about grammar' either never happened at all, or else took place through English. From a perspective which emphasises maximising pupil exposure to 'comprehensible input', this represents a constraint on pupils' potential communicative FL experience in the classroom. It was therefore felt useful for the purposes of the Communicative Interaction project to study more closely at least one attempt to tackle an activity of this type through French, if only to learn more about the nature of the obstacles which make FL use unpopular for this purpose.

SUMMARY DESCRIPTION

Teacher G at Bloomfield High School agreed to attempt the explanation of a 'grammar point' to an S1 class through the medium of French. This teacher had a high commitment to classroom communication through French, but was normally an adherent of the 'inductive' approach to teaching grammar. The point selected was the introduction of the written forms of some parts of the verb system: viz, the present tense of -*er* verbs, with *je*, *tu* and *vous*. This activity was attempted in the third term of S1, with a mixed ability class of 29 pupils. Presentation of the written forms took place towards the end of an hour-long lesson, which had begun with extensive oral practice designed as a lead up to it.

This oral practice phase took about 35 minutes. It comprised a mixture of practice and communicative FL activities (predominantly the former), some whole class, and some involving pair work. Together, these preliminary oral activities provided pupils with varied practice in hearing and producing the forms:

j'aime	*je déteste*	*je joue*
tu aimes	*tu détestes*	*tu joues*
vous aimez	*vouz détestez*	*vous jouez*

The teacher began the section of the lesson dealing with the written forms by reminding pupils of the concept 'verb', which they exemplified orally in English and in French.

Together the teacher and pupils cooperated in building up on the blackboard the forms of *aimer*, *détester* and *jouer* previously practised orally. The spelling rule was deduced from these three examples. From further verbs suggested by the pupils, four were selected (*allumer, ouvrir, fermer*), to which pupils were asked to apply the rule in writing. The remaining time was spent in completion of this written task; the teacher circulated among the pupils, spending time notably with a group who had apparently failed to follow the initial presentation, and with an infrequent attender.

To assess pupils' grasp of the point taught, their written efforts were not discussed or corrected in class, but collected and retrospectively assessed. Their performance was judged as follows:

Successfully completed task: 21 pupils

Task not completed, but work done
showed comprehension: 3 pupils

Performance on task suggested non-
comprehension: 5 pupils

COMMENTARY

Teacher G completed the lesson more or less as planned, sustaining French use (and a high level of pupil involvement) throughout. She considered the pupils' level of performance on the written task to be satisfactory, and not significantly different from that to be expected had English been used.

Nonetheless, some difficulties did arise in Teacher G's lesson, which it appeared difficult to resolve satisfactorily through French. Firstly, the teacher's introduction of the abstract concept of a 'verb' relied heavily on the pupils' existing understanding which equated a verb with a 'doing word'. This led to difficulties with exemplification, as the following extract shows:

TG   ...Alors, on va maintenant, on va regarder les verbes. Qu'est-ce qu c'est, un verbe? Un verbe.

P   A doing word!

TG   Oui, c'est ça, c'est ça. Un verbe, oui. Alors, Pauline, tu peux me donner des verbes en anglais? Un verbe en anglais. Pardon, Noreen. Je me trompe toujours! Pardon, je m'excuse. Noreen, tu peux me donner un verbe en anglais?

P   Anglais emm - hockey?

TG   Ça c'est un verbe? Hockey?

P   Oh! run.

TG   Run, oui, ça c'est un verbe. Tu peux me donner un verbe en anglais?

P   Jump!

TG   Jump, oui, oui.

(PUPILS GIVE FURTHER EXAMPLES)

P   Shout

TG Shout, *oui, c'est ça, c'est ça. Alors - ah, ah, ah, ça c'est trop facile. Ça c'est facile. Maintenant des verbes en anglais - en français, pardon! Des verbes en français! Est-ce que -*

P   *Na - na - natation!*

TG *Ça c'est un verbe? La natation, c'est un verbe?*

P   It's what you do, you swim!

TG *Oui, mais la natation, c'est* 'swimming', 'swimming'. *La natation', c'est* 'swimming'...

P   *Lève-toi!*

TG *Lève-toi, oui, ça c'est un verbe*

(PUPILS GIVE FURTHER EXAMPLES)

P   *Joue*

TG *Joue, joue, c'est un verbe, joue?*

P   *Oui.*

TG *Oui, c'est un verbe. Joue, c'est un verbe. Alors, 'aime' aussi, ça c'est un verbe, n'est-ce pas ? 'Aime', 'aime'. J'aime le français. Aime, j'aime l'anglais. Aime, c'est un verbe.*

P   *Non!*

TG *Je te dis, oui, c'est un verbe! C'est un verbe. Ne t'inquiète pas, c'est un verb...* (etc)

While sticking to French, the teacher seemed to have no means open to her other than exemplification, in attempting to develop the pupils' understanding of what is a verb and what is not.

The second major obstacle arose in trying to convey to pupils the precise details of the writing task they were to undertake as a consolidation exercise. After plentiful written demonstrations on the blackboard (by pupil volunteers as well as by the teacher herself), Teacher G gave instructions for the individualised task. During these instructions she again referred to the board:

TG *Sur - sur la feuille que vous avez, sur le papier, vous allez écrire... 'J'écoute'. Et aussi la question, 'tu -'... Et aussi la question, 'vous'. Vous allez écrire... 'Je', 'tu', 'vous'. Vous allez écrire aussi, 'je' avec 'ouvre', 'tu' avec 'ouvre', 'vous' avec 'ouvre'. Et vous allez faire 'j'' avec 'allume', 'tu' avec 'allume', 'vous' avec 'allume'. Hein? Il faut trouver, il faut trouver les lettres. Tu n'as pas compris?*

P	*Oui*
TG	*Tu as compris?*
PP	*Non.*
TG	*Tu n'as pas compris?*
PP	*Oui! Non!*
TG	*Oui ou non?*
P	*Non!*
TG	*Tu n'as pas compris. Alors. On va - on va refaire avec 'aime'. Qu'est-ce que j'écris ici? Qu'est-ce que j'écris? 'Aime'*
PP	*A - I - M - E*
T	*E. Et la question 'tu'?*
PP	*A - I - M - E - S*
TG	*Voilà, et la question 'vous'?*
PP	*A - I - M - E - Z*
TG	*Vous allez faire ça avec toutes - tous les verbes. Hmm? Les trois parties avec tous les verbes. Tu as compris? Tu as compris? Qui n'a pas compris? Qui n'a pas compris? Tu n'as pas compris, Caroline? Non? Bon...*

At this point the teacher left most of the class to get on with the task, and went to the assistance of 'Caroline' and her group (this extra help was still given in French). Observation suggested that at this stage by no means everyone had grasped what was required; however, classroom custom and seating arrangements were such as to foster peer tuition, and it seemed the high rate of task completion was partly due to the preparedness of pupils who had grasped the rule to explain the task to others. Unsurprisingly, this pupil-pupil support was all English-medium, as far as could be determined.

Once again, therefore, it seemed to be the conveyance of abstract and decontextualised information (such as the arbitrary convention of a spelling rule) which caused difficulties for FL use. It seems likely that it is the inevitable concentration of such topics inherent in metalinguistic discussion which makes teachers fight shy of FL use for 'grammar explanations'. The success of Teacher G's lesson, both in terms of pupil involvement and performance outcomes, was the carefully-planned achievement of a skilled and flexible communicator; and even she, as we have seen, was forced at certain moments to compromise on the quality of information being transmitted, in order to sustain the FL-medium character of the lesson.

Skill training study

INTRODUCTION

The term 'skill training' was used within the project to refer to activities in which pupils are taught how to perform one of a number of simple 'life skills' such as everyday computation, or the use of maps, charts or timetables. Examples of such activities witnessed during the Stage 2 period of general observation included teaching pupils how to use a town plan; how to read a railway time table; and how to use the 24 hour clock.

During the first phase of Stage 2, any skill training activities which occurred were almost always handled through the medium of English. As with the background grammar studies, it was felt an action research investigation could help establish what foundation there was for the unpopularity of skill training as an occasion for communicative FL use.

SUMMARY DESCRIPTION

Teacher L at Jespersen Academy undertook to carry out a 'skill training' activity through the medium of French as the focus of an action research study, with an S2 class of 32 pupils (a top set in the first term of S2). The topic selected was the conversion of kilometres into miles.

The lesson involved a preliminary statement of the purpose of the activity (*Calculer les distances*), followed by a brief rehearsal of numbers between 100 and 500. The teacher then presented the idea of distances in Scotland being measured in miles (with the aid of a **roadmap** and the *Book of the Road*), while distances in France are normally measured in kilometres (the *Guide de la Route* was referred to).

A **blackboard diagram** was then drawn to illustrate the length relationship between one mile and one kilometre. The blackboard was used again to support a verbal explanation of the numerical formula to be used to convert kilometres into miles (the teacher **wrote up the formula** $\div$ 8, x 5). The teacher then worked through several contextualised examples of its application to longer and shorter distances, again writing up the figures. Lastly, a **work-sheet** was distributed to the pupils, which they completed partly during the 'target' lesson, and partly on the following day.

PUPIL QUESTIONNAIRE

In the last few moments of the lesson the pupils wrote the answers to three questions read to them by the researcher. The questions, and pupil answers, were as follows:

1. How long did it take you to work out what Teacher L was talking about in this lesson?

Knew immediately	7 pupils
A few minutes	24 pupils
Quite a while	1 pupil

2. What is the rule for converting kms to miles?

÷ 8, x 5	31 pupils
x 5, ÷ 8	1 pupil

3. Did you know this rule before today?

Yes	10 pupils
No	22 pupils

COMMENTARY

Teacher L was completely successful in sustaining FL use throughout this activity. She felt the lesson had been effective in ensuring pupil understanding of the rule (a view confirmed by their performance on the specially prepared worksheet, as well as on the brief questionnaire reported above). The following extract includes the initial presentation of the arithmetical rule. The teacher's FL talk was supported by reference to the blackboard:

TL   *Okay, vous comprenez?... Une mille, c'est long, mais un kilomètre, c'est plus court... Pour changer les distances, pour changer les distances en kilomètres en milles, il y a un système, un méthode très facile, très simple. Qu'est-ce que vous faites? Vous prenez un exemple, par example la distance entre Paris - Lyon. Voilà Paris... Voilà Lyon. La distance entre Paris et Lyon, c'est à peu pres... Quatre cents kilomètres, okay? Alors pour changer quatre cents kilomètres en milles... Ça, qu'est-ce que vous faites? Deux choses... Numéro un. Vous divisez. Vous divisez ça par huit. Divisez... par huit. Okay? Huit, divisez, résultat... okay? Résultat, c'est cinquante... Deuxième partie... Vous multipliez ça... par cinq... Vous multipliez ça par cinq, résultat... Okay? Alors voilà... Quatre cents kilomètres, c'est deux cent cinquante milles. Okay? Encore une fois. Très simple... Pour avoir la distance en milles, vous divisez par huit, okay? Voilà le résultat... Après, vous multipliez par cinq, c'est ça. Donc quatre cents kilomètres, voilà, en milles, c'est deux cents cinquante milles. Vous avez compris? Oui?... Vous avez compris, oui? Ça va? Bon. Un autre exemple (etc)*

As this extract suggests, the talk in this lesson was rather onesided throughout, with hardly any pupil contributions during the whole-class presentation. The teacher said this was partly due to the personality and previous experience of this particular S2 class (they, and she, were new to extensive classroom FL use!). However, comprehension was assured without overt, interactive pupil involvement. It seemed to the teacher that an important element in promoting this was the fact that the 'rule' being taught could be written in language-free, mathematical notation. While this certainly helped, her own language presentation, involving flexible use of appropriate simplification strategies as well as copious exemplification, seemed also to be an important contributing factor.

CONCLUSION

This handful of studies could yield no more than a few pointers regarding the likely costs and benefits of conducting content-orientated activities through French. They suggest that at least some informational activity types are feasible at S1/S2 level, if carefully planned and implemented by teachers skilled in simplification and communication strategies; but they also permit the identification of several likely difficulties and disadvantages. These include limitations to the depth and subtlety with which more abstract topics can be treated; increased time requirements; and the possible restriction of pupil contributions to the discourse into a narrow stream of comprehension checks. More generally, as appeared in at least one study, it is possible seriously to miscalculate the level of linguistic difficulty, and so expose pupils to extended bursts of incomprehensible input. Experience in other cultures of 'immersion' education, where an L2 is relied on completely for the teaching of academic content of all kinds, still suggests that information-orientated activities could play a greater role in broadening teachers' currently narrow repertoire of communicative FL activities. But these five studies remind us of some pitfalls.

CHAPTER 5

LINGUISTIC FEATURES OF TEACHER FL TALK

INTRODUCTION

The last three chapters have analysed the classroom data collected during Stage 2 at the segmental or 'activity' level, discussing entire teaching/learning episodes which were characterised as (mainly) communicative FL, practice FL or L1-medium. It was recognised, however, that the detail of interaction within any given lesson segment might not conform precisely to such overall characterisations.

The next three chapters of this report consider various subsegmental aspects of classroom language, relevant to the provision of communicative FL experience for pupils. Particular attention is paid to the language of the teacher.

TEACHER TALK AND THE COURSEBOOK SYLLABUS

All the teachers observed during Stage 2 were attempting to develop active pupil mastery of a specified coursebook language syllabus. It was therefore to be expected that the language material of whatever coursebook unit was being studied would occur frequently in the teachers' own speech, as they modelled, reinforced and corrected the target forms of the syllabus, during the practice FL segments which predominated in most classrooms. This indeed turned out to be the case, across all four schools. However, most of the teachers involved in the observational phase added a considerable increment to the syllabus list in their own classroom talk.

Teacher talk: Palmer High School

During the Stage 2 observational visits, the S1 classes at Palmer High School were working on a unit of *Tour de France* Stage 1, *La famille Garnier* (published version). The S2 classes were working on a Stage 2 unit, *Circuit touristique* (pilot version). Much of the French spoken by teacher and pupils consisted in rehearsal of the language syllabus of these units; this was the case for a very high proportion of the FL utterances produced by the pupils.

The structure and lexis of the FL spoken by all four teachers, however, and thus provided as 'input' for the pupils, consistently went considerably beyond the language syllabus of *Tour de France* up to the points reached by the S1 and S2 groups. For example, while the *Tour de France* syllabus had systematically introduced no tense forms other than the present up to the point reached by the S2 classes, all the teachers regularly made use of perfect and imperfect tense forms in addition to present tense forms. They all commonly used *aller* + infinitive to express futurity, and a range of constructions with modal auxiliaries (*vouloir, pouvoir, devoir, falloir*). Complex sentences were produced occasionally by the S1 teachers (e.g. *Si on veut faire marcher le projecteur, qu'est-ce qu'on demande?*: TA), more commonly by the S2 teachers. More of the pronominal system was in use than was indicated in the syllabus (e.g. *on*, direct object pronouns and indirect object pronouns were all noted in the speech of all teachers); a wider range of adverb forms was noted (*puis, alors, maintenant, hier*, etc). Some language functions proposed in the syllabus occurred with alternative exponents additional to those suggested in the syllabus; for example, 'commands' were commonly realised using declarative forms as well as imperative forms, in all classrooms (e.g. *Tournez à la page 6! Colette, tu lis l'exemple!*: TA)

The detailed analysis of the audiorecorded Stage 2 lesson material which would have been necessary to provide a comprehensive picture of the range of vocabulary used by the teachers was beyond the resources of the research project. However, some light was shed on the question of lexical range by analysis of the verb forms recorded in the observer's detailed notes on the Stage 2 lessons. Table 5.1 lists those French verbs, any part of which was noted as having been produced by the teachers at Palmer High School during these lessons. The fact that this analysis was based only on notes means it is likely to underrepresent the range of verbs in use. However, the table shows that parts of 62 different verbs appeared in the notes taken at S1 level, of which 33 were to be found in the *Tour de France* 'active' syllabus (Stage 1 Pupil's Book, pp 55-56). The S1 teachers (Teachers A and D) were thus strikingly 'ahead' of the pupil syllabus in lexical as well as structural terms; although three full units of Stage 1 remained to be taught, they had already introduced in their own speech a majority of the verbs figuring on the syllabus list, as well as many others which did not appear on it at all. It also appears from Table 5.1 that the range of verbs in use in the two S1 classes was very similar. This similarity may be related partly to the common syllabus, but also partly to the fact that the 'extra' verbs mostly appeared in teacher FL utterances with a managerial function, and the instructions the teachers wished to give were themselves fairly similar.

Table 5.1

Verbs noted in teacher FL talk, Palmer High School

Verb	Used by S1 teacher(s)	Used by S2 teacher(s)	In *Tour de France* Stage 1 Pupils Book Syllabus
accepter	-	+	-
adorer	-	+	+
aider	+	+ +	-
aimer	-	+ +	+
ajouter	-	+ +	-
aller	+ +	+ +	+
allumer	+	+ +	+
s'appeler	+ +	+	+
apporter	-	+ +	-
arriver	-	+	-
s'asseoir	+ +	-	+
attendre	+	+	-
avoir	+ +	+ +	+
baisser	+	-	-
balancer	-	+	-
boire	-	+	+
bouger	+	-	-
se calmer	-	+	-
changer	+ +	+ +	-
chercher	-	+ +	+
choisir	+ +	+ +	-
commencer	+	+ +	-
compléter	-	+	-
comprendre	+ +	+ +	+
compter	-	+	-
continuer	-	+	-
corriger	-	+	-
couvrir	-	+ +	-
crier	+	-	-
croire	-	+	-
danser	-	+	-
décider	-	+	-
demander	+	+ +	-
se dépêcher	+	+	+

Verb	Used by S1 teacher(s)	Used by S2 teacher(s)	In *Tour de France* Stage 1 Pupils Book Syllabus
dessiner	+ +	-	+
détester	-	+	+
deviner	+ +	+ +	-
devoir	-	+	-
dire	+ +	+ +	-
discuter	-	+	-
distribuer	+ +	+ +	+
donner	+ +	+	-
échanger	-	+	-
écouter	+ +	+ +	+
écrire	+ +	+ +	+
entendre	+	-	+
essayer	-	+	-
éteindre	+	-	+
être	+ +	+ +	+
s'excuser	-	+	-
expliquer	+ +	+	-
faire	+ +	+ +	-
faire beau	-	+ +	-
faire du vent	-	+	-
faire mauvais	-	+	-
faire marcher	+ +	+	+
falloir	+ +	+ +	-
fermer	+	+	+
finir	+ +	+ +	-
gagner	-	+ +	-
habiter	+ +	+	+
imaginer	-	+	-
introduire	-	+	-
jouer	-	+ +	-
(se) lever	+	+	+
lire	+	+ +	+
manger	-	+ +	+
manquer	+ +	-	-
marcher	-	+ +	-
marquer	-	+	-
mettre	+ +	+ +	-
monter	-	+	+

Verb	Used by S1 teacher(s)	Used by S2 teacher(s)	In *Tour de France* Stage 1 Pupils Book Syllabus
montrer	-	+	-
nager	-	+ +	-
naître	-	+	-
offrir	+ +	-	-
ôter	-	+	-
oublier	+ +	+ +	+
ouvrir	+	+	+
parler	+ +	+ +	+
partir	-	+	+
passer	+ +	+ +	+
patiner	-	+	-
payer	-	+	-
perdre	-	+	+
photographier	-	+ +	-
plaire	+ +	+ +	-
pleuvoir	-	+	-
plier	-	+	-
porter	-	+ +	-
poser	+ +	+ +	-
pouvoir	+ +	+ +	+
préférer	-	+	+
prendre	+ +	+	+
préparer	-	+	+
prononcer	-	+	-
quitter	-	+ +	-
raconter	-	+	-
ramasser	-	+	-
ranger	+ +	+ +	-
rayer	-	+	-
recommencer	-	+	-
refaire	-	+	-
refuser	+	-	-
regarder	+ +	+ +	+
répéter	+ +	+ +	+
répondre	+ +	-	+
revenir	-	+	-
sauter	-	+	-

Verb	Used by S1 teacher(s)	Used by S2 teacher(s)	In *Tour de France* Stage 1 Pupils Book Syllabus
sonner	+	-	-
sortir	+	+ +	-
suffir	+	+	-
suivre	-	+	-
tailler	+ +	-	-
se taire	-	+	-
téléphoner	-	+	-
tenir	+ +	-	+
tourner	+	+	+
travailler	+	+	+
traverser	-	+ +	+
tricher	-	+	-
trouver	+	-	-
tuer	-	+	-
venir	+	+	+
visiter	-	+ +	-
voir	+	+ +	+
vouloir	+ +	+ +	-

| Total verbs = 127 | Total verbs used by S1 teachers = 62 | Total verbs used by S2 teachers = 112 | Total verbs from *Tde F* Stage 1 syllabus = 45 |

The table shows that the S2 teachers (Teachers B and C) used a substantially wider range of verbs, 112 in all. Just under half these verbs were documented in use at S1 level, and others occurred in the *Tour de France* syllabus up to the point of instruction of the S2 classes. However, a higher proportion than in the case of the S1 teachers was 'individualised' usage, i.e. involved use of verbs outside the syllabus, by a single teacher only. The greater variety can partly be accounted for by the greater range of uses to which French was put at S2 level in this school; while a large number of 'individualised' verb forms occurred in utterances with a managerial purpose, some occurred in the course of pedagogic exposition, and some in 'social' interaction between teacher and pupils.

Teacher talk: Bloomfield High School

Tour de France was also in use in the classes observed during the Stage 2 observational visits to Bloomfield High School. The S1 classes (taught by Teachers G and H) were working on the same unit of Stage 1 (*La famille Garnier*: published version). The S2 classes (taught by Teachers E and F) were seen taking a Stage 2 attainment test and then embarking on the unit *Circuit touristique* (pilot version).

As at Palmer High School, much of the French spoken in the classroom by both teachers and pupils consisted in rehearsal of the language syllabus of these units of *Tour de France* intended for active mastery by the pupils. However, the FL utterances of the teachers again sometimes went considerably beyond this 'core' syllabus, in both structural complexity and lexical range.

As an illustration of the lexical range of the Bloomfield teachers' FL talk, Table 5.2 again lists all FL verbs of which some part was noted by the observer as having been used by at least one of the teachers.

This table shows that, as at Palmer High School, the Bloomfield S1 teachers were already using a range of vocabulary substantially wider than that of the *Tour de France* pupil materials. Not yet half way through Stage 1, they were already using over 70 per cent of the Pupil's Book syllabus, plus a further 40 'extra' verbs.

Comparison of the usage of the S1 and S2 teachers produced a different picture from that found at Palmer High School, however. The number and range of verbs noted in the S1 and S2 teacher talk were in this case strikingly similar; 57 verbs (or over 70 per cent of the S2 lists) were used at both levels. Of this shared 'core' half appears in the Stage 1 Pupil's Book syllabus; the rest originated at both levels in FL use for managerial purposes.

Analysis of the range of grammatical structures noted in the speech of S1 and S2 teachers showed similarities also. For example, all the teachers used the perfect tense, and the *futur proche* (*aller* + infinitive); but only one (S1) teacher was noted to use both of these more than ten times each. The only other tense noted more than once (other than the present) was the imperfect; one or two instances of its use were noted for both S1 teachers, and one S2 teacher.

The infrequent incidence of complex sentences (e.g. involving *si... ...ce que...*) was similar for S1 and S2, as was the use of a wider pronoun system than that suggested by the syllabus (for example, *on*, *nous*, and various indirect object pronouns occurred occasionally at both levels). No instances of use of subjunctive forms were noted at either level.

This close similarity in FL usage at S1 and S2 levels was somewhat unexpected. One possible explanation derived from the fact that the teachers all described themselves at the time as being in a stage of transition, and moving towards increased levels of FL usage.

Table 5.2

Verbs noted in teacher FL talk, Bloomfield High School

Verb	Used by S1 teacher(s)	Used by S2 teacher (s)	In *Tour de France* Stage 1 Pupils book Syllabus
aimer	-	+	+
aller	+ +	+ +	+
allumer	-	+	-
s'appeler	+ +	-	+
arrêter	-	+	+
arriver	+	-	-
s'asseoir	+ +	+ +	+
avoir	+ +	+ +	+
avoir besoin	+	-	-
boire	-	+	+
se calmer*	+	-	-
changer	+	+ +	
chercher	+	+ +	+
choisir	+	+	-
commencer	+	+ +	-
comprendre	+ +	+ +	+
compter	+	-	-
continuer	+	+ +	-
corriger*	+	-	-
danser	+	-	
demander	+	+	-
se dépêcher	+	+	+
dessiner	-	+	+
détester*	-	+	+
dire	+ +	+ +	-
distribuer*	+ +	+	+
donner	+	+	-
écouter	+ +	+ +	+
écrire	+ +	+ +	+
effacer	+	-	-
enlever	+	+	-
entendre	+ +	+	-
entrer	-	+	-
essayer	-	+	-

Verb	Used by S1 teacher(s)	Used by S2 teacher(s)	In *Tour de France* Stage 1 Pupils Book Syllabus
être	+ +	+ +	+
expliquer	+	-	-
faire	+	+ +	-
faire beau	-	+	-
" chaud	+	+	-
" du brouillard	-	+	-
" du vent	-	+	-
" froid	-	+	-
" marcher	-	+ +	+
falloir	+	-	-
fermer	+ +	+	+
finir	+	+ +	-
habiter	+ +	+ +	+
jouer	+	+ +	-
laver	-	+	-
(se) lever	+ +	+ +	+
lire	+ +	+ +	+
manger	+	+	+
marcher	-	+	-
(se) mettre	+ +	+ +	-
monter	+	+ +	+
montrer	-	+	-
nettoyer	+	-	-
oublier	+ +	+ +	+
ouvrir	+ +	+ +	+
parler	+	+ +	+
passer	+	+	+
penser	-	+	-
perdre	+	-	+
photographier	-	+	-
pleuvoir	+	+	-
poser	+	+	-
pouvoir	-	+ +	+
prendre	+	+	+
préparer	+	+	-
préférer	-	+	+
quitter	-	+	-
ramasser	+	+	-

Verb	Used by S1 teacher(s)	Used by S2 teacher (s)	In *Tour de France* Stage 1 Pupils book Syllabus
ranger	+ +	+ +	-
recommencer	+	-	-
regarder	+ +	+ +	+
rendre	+	-	-
répéter	+	+	+
répondre	+ +	+ +	+
se retourner	-	+	-
se réveiller	+	+	-
réviser*	+	+	-
savoir	+ +	+ +	+
sortir	+	+ +	-
souligner*	-	+	-
suffir*	+ +	+	-
se taire	+	+	-
tenir	+ +	+	-
tirer	+	+ +	+
(se) tourner	+	+ +	+
travailler	+ +	+ +	+
tricher*	+	-	-
(se) trouver	+	+	-
venir	+	+ +	+
voir	+ +	+ +	+
vouloir	+	+ +	-

Total verbs = 95	Total verbs used by S1 Ts = 72	Total verbs used by S2 Ts = 80	Total verbs from *T de F* Stage 1 syllabus = 40

* = verb not listed in *Le français fondamental*

They also reported such shifts as being more easily made with a new class of S1 entrants, than with classes having established expectations for teachers' language use. Thus the similar levels of FL with S1 and S2 classes in 1981-82 may have been one phase in a movement to higher all round levels of FL use. Alternatively, they may be evidence of a 'plateau effect': having established a set of basic FL routines, the teachers may have been unable or unwilling to develop them. But either explanation is speculative.

Teacher talk: Sweet Grammar School

The Stage 2 observational visits to Sweet Grammar School involved one S1 class, working on Unit 2 of the *Eclair* course, and two S2 classes working on Unit 6. Once again the structural complexity and lexical range of the teachers' French outran the coursebook syllabus, to varying degrees. Table 5.3 shows the range of verbs noted from the teachers' FL talk. As before, they were all using a range of vocabulary in their own speech which was substantially wider than that of the *Eclair* syllabus. Hardly any verbs have been introduced by Unit 2 of this course - yet the S1 teacher (Teacher K) used parts of 32 different ones. Those she used were almost all noted also in the utterances of at least one S2 teacher. The S2 teachers (Teachers I and J) used totals of 57 and 72 respectively; their choice of vocabulary showed more individuality, with 53 verbs being used by one or other of these teachers, but not by both. They also substantially outran the *Eclair* wordlist up to and including Unit 6.

More apparent influence from the syllabus could be detected in the range of grammatical structures being employed with some frequency by the teachers in their own speech. Thus the verb form most frequently used by Teacher K (other than present tense and imperative forms) was the conditional *voudrais/voudrait*; this was being actively taught as the slot-and-filler exponent for 'asking politely for...'. However, she used *futur proche*, perfect and imperfect tense forms on one or two occasions only. On the other hand, the S2 teachers both used the *futur proche* with greater frequency than any other verb form apart from present tense and imperative forms; again, this was related to several 'target functions' for the unit on which they were working, and the preceding one. Apart from this shared emphasis, however, the FL spoken by the S2 teachers differed somewhat in general structural

Table 5.3

Verbs noted in teacher FL talk, Sweet Grammar School

Verb	Used by S1 teacher	Used by S2 teacher(s)
aimer	-	+ +
aller	+	+ +
(s') appeler	-	+ +
(s') arrêter	-	+ +
s'asseoir	-	+ +
avoir	+	+ +
se calmer	-	+ +
changer	+	-
chercher	+	-
commencer	-	+ +
comprendre	+	+ +
continuer	+	+
corriger	-	+
connaître	-	+ +
danser	-	+
décider	-	+
demander	-	+
se dépêcher	+	+
dessiner	+	+ +
deviner	-	+
devoir	-	+
dire	+	+ +
distribuer	+	+
donner	+	+ +
dormir	-	+
écouter	+	+ +
écrire	+	+ +
enlever	-	+
entendre	-	+
entrer	-	+
épeler	-	+
essayer	-	+
être	+	+ +
étudier	-	+
s'excuser	-	+
exister	-	+

Verb	Used by S1 teacher	Used by S2 teacher(s)
expliquer	-	+
s'éveiller	-	+
faire	+	+
faire beau	-	+
faire chaud	-	+ +
faire du camping	-	+ +
faire de l'équit	-	+
faire du ski	-	+ +
faire du soleil	-	+
faire du vélo	-	+
faire froid	-	+
falloir	-	+
fermer	+	+ +
finir	+	+ +
gagner	-	+
identifier	-	+
imaginer	-	+
indiquer	-	+
s'installer	-	+
jouer	-	+ +
(se) lever	-	+
lire	-	+
laisser	-	+
manger	-	+ +
manquer	+	+ +
mentionner	-	+
nager	-	+ +
offrir	-	+
ôter	+	-
oublier	+	-
ouvrir	+	+ +
parler	-	+ +
(se) passer	-	+ +
partir	-	+
pleuvoir	-	+
poser	+	+
pouvoir	-	+ +
préférer	-	+
prendre	-	+ +
quitter	-	+

Verb	Used by S1 teacher	Used by S2 teacher(s)
ranger	+	-
regarder	+	+ +
rendre	+	+
répéter	+	+
représenter	-	+
rester	-	+ +
se retourner	-	+ +
se réveiller	-	+
savoir	+	+ +
signifier	-	+ +
sortir	-	+ +
suffir	-	+
suivre	-	+
tourner	+	+ +
travailler	-	+ +
venir	-	+
vérifier	-	+
visiter	-	+
voir	+	+ +
vouloir	+	+ +

| Total verbs = 96 | Total verbs used by S1 T = 32 | Total verbs used by S2 Ts = 92 |

complexity. Teacher J regularly used items such as perfect and imperfect tense forms, and modal verbs followed by infinitives, and also occasionally used complex sentence patterns (e.g. with *...qui...*, *ce que*.... Teacher I only occasionally used any of these items, and was once or twice noted to avoid them in contexts where this seemed to involve breaking the rules of 'normal' conversation, e.g.:

TI *Neil, l'année dernière, l'année dernière...*
P   *(...)*
TI Last year, *l'année dernière, <u>où vas-tu passer</u> les grandes vacances?*
P   *Je vais en Angleterre, et en Belgique, et en Autriche.*

Teacher talk: Jespersen Academy

At the time of the Stage 2 observational visits, the relationship between the languages syllabus of *Tricolore*, and the French used actively by the teachers at Jespersen, was substantially different from that observed in the *Tour de France* and *Eclair*-using schools. As we have seen, in the three other departments, the French spoken by the teachers seemed consistently richer than that of the syllabus intended for pupil mastery. In the *Tricolore*-based lessons at Jespersen this was not the case. Exceptionally, at this school both teachers (Teachers L and M) were observed at both S1 and S2 levels. In the S1 lessons, the set of verbs noted by the observer as having been used in the teachers' speech was almost identical with those occurring in the pupil materials. At S2 level, the match was less precise; about 40 per cent of the verbs used by each teacher did not occur in the materials for the relevant unit of work. However, in each case the absolute number of verbs noted as used by the teachers (28 and 39 respectively) was somewhat smaller than the absolute number occurring in the pupil materials (just over 40 verbs).

The range of grammatical structures used by the different teachers gave a similar picture. Prominent in the French spoken by the Jespersen teachers were the 'target' structures of the syllabus of the current unit, intended for active pupil mastery (e.g. at S2 level *pouvoir* + infinitive, and at S1 level, *il fait beau/chaud*, etc); structures not yet actively taught were strikingly rare. The overall impression was one of self-censorship (conscious or unconscious), with the teachers limiting their own FL production to those structures and vocabulary which the pupils might reasonably be expected to produce at this early stage.

At the time of the Stage 2 observational visits, the teachers at Jespersen expressed doubt as to the feasibility of extensive FL use for classroom management, and the effective restriction of their own FL talk to 'syllabus speak' could clearly be related to this; for all but very simple organising instructions, at this time, these teachers were communicating management messages through English. However, a striking change had come about by the time of the interventionist visits, which took place at Jespersen almost a full year later. By this time both teachers had become committed to promoting FL use as the norm for classroom communication and were using French extensively for managerial purposes. Due to the different form of the interventionist visits, an equivalent detailed analysis of linguistic features of their FL talk was not possible; it was, however, clear that by this time their talk resembled that at the other three schools much more closely, in its structural and lexical range.

BEYOND 'SYLLABUS SPEAK'

Overall, the 'enrichment' of teacher FL talk by comparison with their coursebook language syllabuses appeared to come about largely as a result of the teachers' commitment to the use of French for classroom management purposes. A further source of enrichment at least in some S2 classes seemed to be the use of French for substantive academic content, and for informal social interaction with pupils.

One further general condition seemed to apply for teachers to liberate themselves from the notion that 'syllabus speak' is the only proper form of FL input. This was the realisation that expectations regarding pupil FL output could be 'uncoupled' from the level of complexity of the teachers' own FL talk. These teachers were prepared to use the FL extensively themselves, without ambitious expectations for immediate 'rewards' in terms of the quality of pupil FL talk. While there was occasional evidence in pupil talk of the internalisation of forms not yet systematically taught, on the whole their attempts to use such forms were incompletely successful; often, evidence of comprehension was the only immediate return pupils could make to 'reward' the teachers' efforts. On the whole, the teachers did not appear disconcerted by lack of immediate reproduction of 'extracurricular' forms. They usually pushed pupils to produce correct expanded FL forms only for items already systematically taught, and some regularly engaged in extended bilingual interaction with pupils, without pushing them to express personalised messages in French at all. The teachers seemed to sustain their personal commitment to speaking French largely in the belief that extensive exposure to FL teacher talk would be of benefit to pupils in the longer rather than shorter term.

SIMPLIFICATION IN TEACHER TALK

While teacher talk in FL-managed classrooms went considerably beyond 'syllabus speak', the teachers nonetheless took careful account of their interlocutors' limitations as far as comprehension was concerned, consistently adapting their French in ways likely to make it more accessible to their pupils.

One broad overall technique was that of 'topic avoidance'; as we saw in Chapter 4, teachers generally did not tackle through French any topic seen as abstract, cognitively demanding, or heavily loaded with new information content. Within the topic areas judged suitable for handling through French, the teachers who were most successful in sustaining FL use also employed a wide range of 'simplification strategies' in the moment-to-moment planning and realisation of their talk.

These strategies emerge most strikingly where direct comparisons could be made between teacher talk in English and in French. The following extracts are drawn from the action research study Background 1, described in Chapter 4, in which Teacher A taught the same lesson about tourist Paris to two different S1 classes, one in each language:

(HOW TO BEHAVE ON A BUS: Teacher's commentary on a slide showing a bus and bus stop)

(ENGLISH VERSION)

TA   *Emm, if you've got one of the yellow tickets, the* tickets de métro, *you can use that on the bus. If you've got one of these* (holds up ticket), *when you come into the bus here, there's a machine on your left, and you put it in the machine, which emm cancels your ticket. If you don't have a ticket, you pay the driver there.*

(French version)

TA   *Alors vous avez besoin d'un ticket de métro... (...) Si j'ai un*

> *ticket - (holds up ticket) ...Alors c'est comme pour le métro. Là c'est marqué 'Métro/Autobus'. Alors si vous avez un ticket comme ça, vous montez dans l'autobus, et à gauche là il y a une machine. Tout le monde comprend? Il y a une machine. Alors on prend le ticket - on met le ticket dans la machine, comme ça (gestures), et ça marque - la machine marque le ticket. Tout le monde comprend?*
P   *Oui*
TA   *Alors, si tu n'as pas de ticket, if faut payer au conducteur là. Il faut payer... Tout le monde comprend?*

These extracts illustrate several of the simplification strategies regularly employed by the French-using teachers. The French utterances are short by comparison with those in English, and their structure is more analytic; propositions are usually expressed one at a time. The French extract is more redundant, and contains fewer pro-forms (e.g. nouns are less likely to be replaced by pronouns). It is also more dependent on the extra-linguistic context, and on the teacher's non-verbal behaviour (deictic gestures and miming of actions). Lastly, the teacher seeks positive indications of comprehension by explicitly questioning (*Tout le monde comprend?*). Other characteristic features of the talk which cannot be documented in print were heightened intonation and stronger stress patterns, slower speech with more frequent pausing, and clearer articulation.

Most of these simplification strategies characteristic of teacher FL talk have also been noted by other researchers studying registers such as 'foreigner talk' (native speaker informal talk to L2 leaners: e.g. Hatch, 1979). The teachers' FL speech also shared some characteristics with 'mother talk' (the speech of caretakers with young children: e.g. Snow and Ferguson, eds., 1977). As in mother-child interaction, a set of language **routines** had become established in the language of the FL-managed classrooms (to do with activities such as calling the roll, correcting homework, and organising the physical environment). Such familiar linguistic routines provided a basis for development by **'platforming'** (building on established routines and social knowledge to extend linguistic knowledge). Thus in the following example, familiarity with the kind of things teachers say in certain contexts guides pupil guesses as to the meaning of a new phrase:

TG   *Oui?*
P   *Emm... j'ai - j'ai oublié mon livre...*

TG   *Bon. Heureusement tu n'en as pas besoin. Tu n'en as pas besoin.* What do you think I am saying, *Tu n'en as pas besoin?*

P   It doesn't matter

P   You don't need it

TG   *Oui, c'est ça.* You don't need it, *tu n'en as pas besoin.* (etc) (S1 class)

The teachers also used a procedure akin to the **expansions** characteristic of caretakers' speech (where the adult echoes in full 'correct' form the non-standard utterances of the child); in the teachers' case, they echoed in FL and L1 or interlanguage utterances of their pupils (though usually insisting on pupil self-correction only for structures of the 'official' syllabus). For example:

P   Miss

TG   *Oui?*

P   *Eh, moi déteste...* homework

TG   *Je déteste les devoirs, bof, tant pis!* (S1 class)

It might be supposed that the combination of topic avoidance and teacher skill in the use of simplification strategies, while making for short-term communicative effectiveness, might lead to a 'plateau effect' in the FL speech of the classroom teacher. As this chapter has shown, it did appear that some teachers' French hardly developed in complexity or range between the first and third terms of the school year, or between first and second year classes. However, in the brief comparison with mother talk, 'platforming' and 'expansion' have been noted as two features of teacher FL talk tending to disrupt any such equilibrium.

In the next chapter we consider a further important group of strategies which appeared to help the teachers to expand FL competence without sacrificing communicative FL use.

CHAPTER 6

COMMUNICATION AND REPAIR STRATEGIES

INTRODUCTION

One of the most crucial skills involved in sustaining communicative FL use in the classroom must be that of predicting and solving the comprehension difficulties of pupils as they arise. The Stage 2 teachers who were most successful in achieving this did so partly by the avoidance of topics and of activities likely to lead to very dense comprehension difficulties, and partly by simplification strategies of the kind discussed in Chapter 5. However, even within these limits, FL-using teachers committed to the development of their pupils' FL competence must constantly outrun their existing FL resources, and find it necessary to create and consolidate comprehension of new FL items.

TEACHER COMMUNICATION STRATEGIES

All the teachers observed during the Communicative Interaction Project used English at one time or another to solve pupils' comprehension difficulties. However, those who were most successful in maintaining the norm of FL use for classroom communication also used a wide repertoire of other strategies for conveying meaning.

Such 'communication strategies' are not unique to teachers. Indeed, this term itself has been borrowed from research studies of informal interaction between speakers of unequal competence who do not share a native language (e.g. Tarone, 1980; Faerch and Kasper, 1980, and eds, 1983).

The FL-medium communication strategies commonly occurring in the recorded lessons of this group of teachers, either subsequent to the recognition of a comprehension difficulty, or in order to forestall one, were as follows:

a) **Repetition** - The teacher simply repeats the problematic FL item:

TA   *Si vous commencez là et vous continuez tout droit, trois*
        kilomètres, vous allez arriver à l'autre Arc de Triomphe.
        Vous. comprenez? ... Non?... Ecoutez encore. Alain, si tu
        commences là... et tu continues tout droit... si vous continuez
        tout droit pour trois kilomètres, alors vous arrivez à l'autre
        Arc de Triomphe (Background 1).

b) **Substitution** - The teacher substitutes another, roughly
   equivalent item for the problematic one:

TA   *Alors les Tuileries, c'est un jardin - vous comprenez, un*
        jardin? C'est comme un parc
P   A park
TA   *Oui. Alors c'est un jardin.*

(In this case the teacher has selected as the substitute item a
word with a close English parallel, 'park'. The committed FL-using
teachers made extensive use of such 'cognate' items to facilitate
comprehension.)

c) **Explanation** - The teacher 'explains the meaning' of the item:

TC   *Qui aime ça, patiner à roulettes?*
P   *Madame*
TC   *Oui, Bernard?*
P   *Je ne comprends pas*
TC   *Patiner à roulettes, ça veut dire patiner, mais pas sur la*
        glace, mais avec...
P   *Ah*
TC   *Des chaussures à patiner, mais avec des roulettes comme ça*
        (gestures)
P   *Ah, oui*
TC   *Tu comprends maintenant, oui? Tu aimes ça? Tu aimes ça,*
        patiner à roulettes? (S2 class)

d) **Contrast** - The teacher contrasts the problematic item with
   others which in some way belong to a similar 'set':

TA   *Tout le monde comprend, les autobus? ... (...) alors, si vous*
        voulez faire un tour de Paris, vous pouvez prendre le métro,
        vous pouvez prendre l'autobus normal, Jacques, tu
        comprends? (Background 1)

(Here the problematic item *autobus* is being contrasted with the familiar *métro*.)

e) **Exemplification** - The teacher exemplifies the problematic item:

TJ   *Bon. Ecoute la bande, et écrivez dans votre cahier, en anglais, les mois que vous allez écouter... (...) Tu comprends, Michael?*
P   *Non*
TJ   *Tu ne comprends pas, alors? Ecrivez dans votre cahier en anglais les mots que vous allez entendre. Par exemple, vous entendez 'janvier', et vous écrivez dans votre cahier,* 'January'. (S2 class)

f) **Clue-giving** - The teacher suggests associated concepts:

TA   *Là l'obélisque au milieu, ça c'est de l'Egypte. Vous comprenez, l'Egypte? Vous comprenez, les pyramides? Les pyramides! (...) Alors ça c'est de l'Egypte* (Background 1)

The above list does not exhaust all logical possibilities, though it includes all FL-medium communication strategies commonly used by the teachers in this study. They also used non-linguistic strategies such as mime and gesture; and even when resorting to English, the committed FL-using teachers had some strategies available which largely conserved their own role as consistent FL speakers. These included:

g) **Pupil interpretation** - The teacher (using FL) invites other pupils to supply an L1 equivalent of a problematic FL item:

TK   *(...) Alors voilà un chat, oui?* (pointing to picture) *'Un chat', qu'est-ce que c'est, 'un chat'?*
P1   A cat
TK   *Oui, c'est ça. Alors ehh, et une souris, oui? Il y a une souris -*
P2   A mouse
TK   *Oui* (S1 class)

h) **Teacher interpretation (FL)** - The teacher supplies translations of FL items while sustaining FL use overall:

TA   *Choisis! Tu ne comprends pas 'choisis'? Ça veut dire* 'to choose'.

TB   *Vous comprenez le mot 'histoire'? C'est* 'story' (S2 class)

There were two main types of L1-dominant communication strategies which seemed most threatening to the stability of FL use for classroom management.

i) **Language switching** - The teacher speaks bilingually, repeating messages first expressed in FL immediately in L1:

TG   *Bon, Jason! Jason, voilà! Tu vas préparer le test.* Prepare. *Voilà. Jean, tu as fait le test?* Have you done the test? *Oui? Bon. Tu m'attends, Jason.* Just wait for me (S1 class)

j) **Interpretation** (L1) - In L1-dominant translation exchanges, the quoted 'problem' item is the only FL heard:

TA   What does *'Parle avec ton partenaire'* mean?

P   (explains in L1)

The following extract from an S2 lesson at Sweet Grammar School illustrates the use of a number of the foregoing strategies in combination, in conveying to pupils the ground rules for a new activity:

TJ   *Bon. Ecoutez. Je vais épeler les noms des mois de l'année. Essayez d'identifier quel mois je vais épeler. Vous ne comprenez pas, non?*

PP   *Non*

TJ   *Non. 'Epeler', par exemple, emm... Carol Wilson. Je vais - je vais épeler son nom. C-A-R-O-L W-I-L-S-O-N. Epeler, qu'est-ce que c'est?*

P2   It's her name

TJ   *Bon, emm, qu'est-ce que je fais?*

P3   (...)

TJ   *Non. Je - un moment. Je vais épeler ehh, son nom. Je vais épeler son nom. R-O-B-B - Bébé! R-O-B-B-I-E F-R-A-S-E-R qu'est-ce que c'est, épeler?*

P4   It's his name in French

TJ   *Oui, mais qu'est-ce que je fais, moi?*

P3   What's your first name?

TJ	*Ecoute. Que signifie, que veut dire le mot 'épéler'?*
P5	It's your full name?
P6	Spelling
TJ	*C'est ça, oui*
P6	Spelling
TJ	Spelling, spelling. *Maintenant je vais épeler les mois de l'année. Vous essayez d'identifier quel mois je vais épeler. Vous comprenez?*
PP	*Non*
TJ	*Identifier -*
P3	*Oui*
TJ	*Qu'est-ce que c'est?*
P3	You give them out and (...) the other guy's name
TJ	*Non, non, non. Je vais épeler les mois de l'année, 'janvier', 'février', 'mars', 'avril', et cétera, les mois de l'année. Moi je vais les épeler!*
P3	Oh, the months
TJ	*Oui. Moi je vais les épeler. C'est à vous d'identifier quel mois je vais épeler. Par exemple, par exemple, moi je dis 'M-A-I'. C'est quel mois?*
P3	May
TJ	*Voilà. Tu as identifié le mois que j'ai épelé. Toi tu as identifié le mois que j'ai épelé. Vous comprenez?*
PP	*Non!*
TJ	*Tu comprends, Susan?*
P7	*Oui, je comprends!*
TJ	*Qu'est-ce que c'est?*
P7	You spell the months and we've got to try and pick the month you're spelling.
TJ	*C'est ça, exactement. Encore une fois, répète!*
P7	You'll spell the months and we've got to pick which month you're spelling
TJ	You've got to -
P7	Try and pick the month you're spelling.
TJ	*Oui. Vous comprenez maintenant?*
PP	*Oui.*
TJ	*Est-ce que vous connaissez le jeu,* 'Name that tune'?
PP	(...)
TJ	'Name that tune'!
P8	Ah, that's brilliant!
TJ	*C'est un programme de télévision, n'est-ce pas?*
PP	*Oui!*
TJ	'Name that tune', *bon. Vous essayez de nommer le mois que je vais épeler.*

P9   'Name that month'!

TJ   *Oui,* 'Name that month'. *Vous êtes prêts? Levez la main! Bon.*
       M-A-

P10   *Mardi - oh, non!*

P11   *Mars!*

TJ   *Mars, oui, c'est ça. Mars, voilà.*

PUPIL REPAIR STRATEGIES

As well as doing all they could to make their own FL talk as
accessible as possible to their pupils through the use of
simplification and repair strategies, some teachers also made a
conscious and systematic effort to equip their pupils to gain some
control of classroom FL interaction. This was most noticeable at
Palmer High School, where the most consistent departmental
commitment to FL use for classroom management purposes was to
be found. Here the teachers concentrated especially on equipping
the pupils with the means to indicate via the FL that they were
having a language problem. At S1 level in particular, as occasion
arose, fairly frequent incidents were observed in which pupils were
explicitly taught phrases such as:

> *Je ne comprends pas*
>
> *Comment est-ce qu'on dit X (en français)?*
>
> *X, Qu'est-ce que ça veut dire?*

The following extract from a lesson taught by Teacher D in Term 1
was recorded at a point when these phrases were not yet familiar:

TD   *Bon alors, ouvrez les livres s'il vous plaît, à la feuille no. 4.*
       Ouvrez les livres. Ouvrez les - Philippe! ... Sans parler s'il
       vous plaît, en silence. Yves, ouvre le livre. Page no. 5, feuille
       no. 4... Dépêche-toi! Hurry up!... *Bon alors, moi je vais poser*
       les questions. Nous sommes tous à table, dans la maison, et
       je vous offre quelque chose à manger. Par exemple, je vous
       offre une pomme, ou une banane. Oui? Et vous choisissez.
       Gisèle, tu as un problème? Oui?

P1   *(...)*

TD   *Alors, comment est-ce qu'on dit* 'I don't understand'?

P1   *Comment est-ce qu'on dit -*

TD   *Non, qu'est-ce que ça veut dire, 'comment est-ce qu'on dit...'?*
       'Comment est-ce qu'on dit...'. Oui? Comment est-ce qu'on dit
       'I don't understand'? *Comment est-ce qu'on dit* 'I have forgotten'?
       On dit, 'j'ai oublié'. Comment est-ce qu'on dit 'I don't have a

pencil'? *On dit, 'je n'ai pas de crayon'. Comment est-ce qu'on dit* 'I don't understand'? *Oui Alain?*

P2   *Je ne comprends pas.*

TD   *C'est ça, je ne comprends pas. Alors Gisèle, tu comprends?*

P1   *Je ne comprends pas.*

TD   *Tu ne comprends pas.* Right, you're nodding your head, saying 'I don't understand'! (laughter) *'Je ne comprends pas'* means 'I don't understand'. *Alors, qui comprend? Oui? Explique, Pierre!*

P3   You've got to write down -

TD   *Non! On n'écrit pas, nous parlons.*

P3   You talk!

TD   *Uh-huh*

P3   And you've got to work with your partner, offering something like *'une pomme', 'une banane'.*

TD   *Alors, mais pas toi! Moi, je vais offrir quelque chose. Je suis Madame Garnier.*

P2   (...)

TD   *Non, je suis Mme Garnier.*

P2   We're offering to you?

TD   *Non, j'offre, moi j'offre les choses.*

P2   Ah! You're offering the things to us and we've to choose!

TD   Right, I'm offering to you, and you've to choose whichever one it is! Okay? Okay, boys? *Bon, levez la main, s'il vous plaît. Exemple d'abord! Un gâteau, une pomme? Un gâteau, une pomme? Jean-Paul! Un gâteau, une pomme?*

P4   *Une pomme s'il vous plait -*

TD   *Madame*

P4   *Madame*

TD   *Oui, c'est ça. Bon alors, numéro un...* (etc)

This considerable investment of effort, in a range of FL communication strategies as well as in the teaching of 'repair' phrases to individuals who needed them, obviously delayed the launching of the particular practice FL activity the teacher had in mind. However, presumably as a result of a prior history of incidents of this type, the S2 teachers at Palmer could take it for granted that their pupils had mastered a range of 'repair' phrases to be used as required. Indeed, the general willingness of Palmer pupils to use such phrases suggested that explicit focus on mastery of them had encouraged some realisation that not understanding all of what you hear is a normal part of the FL learning process, rather than an indication of personal failure.

CHAPTER 7

FUNCTIONAL DIFFERENTIATION IN LANGUAGE CHOICE

TEACHERS' CLASSROOM MANAGEMENT LANGUAGE

In the Stage 1 interviews discussed in Chapter 1, teachers distinguished to some extent between different classroom management functions, in terms of those for which they felt it was appropriate to use the target FL, and those for which they would support the use of English. These suggested distinctions were followed up in the analysis of the Stage 2 lesson data. In this section, teachers' language choices for four selected categories of management discourse move are discussed. These are:

1. Organisational instructions
2. Activity instructions
3. Correction and evaluation of pupils' FL performance
4. Disciplinary incidents

Teacher moves in all these categories occurred regularly throughout the S1 and S2 lessons recorded for Stage 2, during and between all types of pedagogic activity (whether communicative FL, practice FL or L1-medium).

1. Organisational instructions

This term was used for those teacher utterances which deal with the physical environment - which tell the pupils how to group themselves, what materials to get out, what page to run to, etc. There are many such utterances in every lesson, and many of them relate to a small set of familiar and predictable routines. They are also frequently supported by visual cues. Together, these characteristics of organisational instructions probably explain why language teachers have always found it relatively easy to realise at least some of them in the target FL. In the Stage 2 observational data, even the teachers at Jespersen Academy used French for a selection of brief, routine organisational instructions (*Asseyez-vous, Tournez à la page X*, etc). At the other schools, most teachers routinely used French for all but the most involved or unusual organisational instructions. For example:

TG   *Bon, Christophe, tu vas travailler avec André s'il te plaît. Change de place. Il n'a pas de partenaire. Toi non plus, tu n'as pas de partenaire, Lorraine? Bon. Voyons. Ah, oui, voilà, tu travailles là. Tu travailles là. Change de place. Bon. Ça y est. Tout le monde a un partenaire, oui? Oui? Bon. Allez-y, au travail, et... voyons... au travail, oui, au travail!* (S1 class, Term 1)

Teachers at S1 level could not assume familiarity with the necessary FL repertoire, and were actively working to develop it:

TH   *Silence la classe! X, Y, distribuez les livres s'il vous plaît. Ecoute bien, la classe! 'Distribuez les livres'.* What does that mean?
PP   Give out the books.
TH   *Ouvrez les livres à la page cinq. Qu'est-ce que ça veut dire, 'page cinq'?* (S1 class, Term 1)

More unusual organisational business in S1 was however sometimes dealt with in L1.

TK   *Russell, ouvre la fenêtre s'il te plaît, et David, la même chose, ouvre la fenêtre. John, ouvre la fenêtre s'il te plaît. Hein?*
P   (...) sellotape
TK   The sellotape is... ah, we'll sort it out at the end of the double period, Daniel. *Bon...* (S1 class, Term 1)

At S2 level, teachers at Palmer, Bloomfield and Sweet could usually assume familiarity with the routine organisation instructions seen being introduced in S1, and regularly used a similar range. However, even in S2 more complex organisational instructions were unusual in French.

2. Activity instructions

'Activity instructions' are those utterances in which the teacher tells the class what the next activity is going to be, and what temporary rules of appropriacy will govern its performance. Only in highly stereotyped teaching can such teacher moves have a routinised character; if the pattern of activities is varied and original, the instructions which introduce them are likely to be correspondingly less 'predictable' by a pupil audience. These are also moves in which the details of the message are likely to be important - 'gist extraction' comprehension levels are inadequate for launching e.g. a complex role play activity.

There thus seem to be *a priori* grounds for thinking that such moves would be more difficult for teachers to make via the FL, as many teachers argued when interviewed for Stage 1.

A majority of the teachers in the Stage 2 sample used English for most activity instructions, even if they regularly used French for other managerial functions. The following example shows switching between French for organisational instructions and English for activity instructions:

TG   *Bon, sortez les livres, sortez les cahiers, vite! Sortez les livres et les cahiers! ...Bon.* Now, I'm going to continue testing those that I haven't tested, and meanwhile, the rest of us we're going to be working, and we're going to start writing some of this work. *Bon. Prenez la page quatre, s'il vous plaît, prenez la page quatre... Bon.* (Reads exercise instructions in L1)(S1 class)

From time to time, teachers who normally used English for activity instructions attempted to introduce an activity in French. Such attempts were accompanied by frequent comprehension checks, and often not fully carried through:

TG   *Bon, vous allez écrire - non. Vous allez faire les exercices. D'abord, vous travaillez avec votre partenaire.* What are you going to do first of all?
P1   Work with your partner
TG   *Oui. Et après, vous allez écrire l'exercice.* What are you going to do afterwards?
P2   Change roles?
TG   *Oui,* but that's not what I said
P3   Write it down
TG   Then write it down. *Oui, oui. Travaillez avec votre partenaire, changez de rôle, et puis, après, écrivéz!* Work with your partner - what am I saying?

(PP re-confirm instructions in L1) (S1 class)

A minority of teachers, those most strongly committed to FL use at all times, regularly attempted activity instructions in French. In Chapter 6, examples of these attempts were quoted (see pp 150-154). These were characterised by extensive use of communication strategies and seemed to require considerable persistence on the part of the teachers concerned.

3.   Correction and evaluation of pupils' FL talk

Unlike most other classroom management moves, teachers' strategies for reacting to their pupils' FL performance varied to some extent with the type of activity taking place. Several teachers reacted (or tried to react) to formal errors made by pupils during communicative FL activities in 'friendly native speaker' fashion, reserving active correction for practice FL activities. All teachers engaged in active correction and explicit evaluation of form at sometime, however, and some did so consistently, regardless of activity type.

Positive evaluation of pupil FL utterances was very commonly expressed by teacher repetition plus a brief FL comment (*Bien, bon, formidable,*' etc). Reactions to formal errors, if felt appropriate, took a variety of forms: modelling of the correct form (by the teacher or another pupil), indicating the existence of a mistake without modelling, giving contrasting examples, or explanation. Such error-handling exchanges typically persisted until the pupil at fault produced a corrected version of his original utterance; they were often conducted entirely through French, as the following examples show:

(CONTRASTING EXAMPLE & MODELLING)

(Teacher E is running a Q/A flashcard drill)

TE	...*Nous avons quatre filles ici. La question? Qu'est-ce que c'est?*
P1	*Qu'est-ce qu'elles font?*
TE	*Qu'est-ce qu'elles font? Bon. Qu'est-ce qu'elles font?... Oui?*
P2	*Je joue au -*
TE	*Non, non. Ca c'est 'Qu'est-ce que tu fais?', hein? 'Je joue'. Qu'est-ce qu'elles font?*
P2	*Elles jouent...basket.*
TE	*Elles jouent -.*
P2	...Netball!

TE   *Non, basket - au netball, oui. Au basket, au basket. 'Elles jouent au basket', répète.*
P2   *Elles jouent au basket.*
TE   *Elles jouent au basket. Qu'est-ce qu'elles font?* (etc) (S2 class)

(INDICATING MISTAKE, NO MODELLING)

P   *Je voudrais un raisin*
TK   *Un raisin?*
P   *Un kilo de raisins!*
TK   *Un kilo de raisins. Alors, voilà un kilo de raisins* (S1 class)

(EXPLANATION)

(Pupils are questioning each other)

P1   *Qui est-ce?*
P2   *C'est Cathérine.*
P1   *Quel age a-t-il?*
TH   *'Il'? 'Il', c'est pour un garçon.*
P1   *Quel age a-t-elle?* (S1 class)

'Explanation' was the only reaction type which offered the choice of using English.

TI   *Et ça, c'est quoi alors?*
P1   *Le automne.*
TI   It starts with an 'A', a vowel, so what happens?
P2   The other vowel gets taken off.
TI   Right. So you say all in one word -
P1   *L'autumn.*
TI   *L'automne, l'automne.*

4.   Disciplinary interventions

The working atmosphere in the classrooms observed for this project was generally good, and the incidence of disruptive pupil behaviour was low. Nonetheless, brief admonitions to *calm down, pay attention* were common in all classes. Several teachers routinely expressed them through French; using phrases such as *Ca suffit, Silence, Ne balance pas sur ta chaise.*

Some teachers were linguistically more ambitious in reacting to routine misdemeanours:

Ne soyez pas si paresseux! (Teacher C)

Je ne suis pas satisfaite, vous refaites ça, et que ça saute!
(Teacher B)

Marie-Claude, je vais te tuer! Il faut écouter, il faut faire attention! (Teacher C)

These same teachers also dealt with some more unusual instances of deviant behaviour in French:

TB	*Sylvestre, s'il te plaît! Tu cesses de jouer aux échecs pendant le cours de français. J'aime bien que les gens jouent aux échecs, mais pas dans les cours! Tu comprends?*
P	*Oui, madame*
TB	*Oui? Alors tu veux me donner ça?* (S2 class)

In two S2 classes observed during Term 3 (after subject choices had been made for the following year), one or two pupils who had decided French was not for them engaged in mildly disruptive behaviour which attracted regular teacher comment and criticism. These pupils were almost always dealt with in English, even by teachers whose commitment to FL use was otherwise high. It seemed that the convention of FL use for disciplinary purposes depended on the prior establishment of a generally positive working atmosphere; even the most strongly committed teachers abandoned it if they felt this atmosphere to be under threat.

PUPIL FL INITIATIVES

The development of pupil FL competence by the route of unconscious acquisition is a slow, incremental process. It could not reasonably be expected, therefore, that teachers' use of French for classroom management purposes would immediately be reciprocated by fluent French from their pupils, for the conveyance of their own 'messages' to do with managerial matters.

At two schools (Jespersen and Sweet), the pupils in fact made hardly any attempt to use French outside the framework of structured pedagogic activities. Their communicative FL use was virtually confined to that required by role plays, games, organised personal discussions, etc; when they needed to speak to the teachers on managerial matters, they always did so in English. At Jespersen during the observational phase, the teachers were also generally using English for such purposes; this was not the case at Sweet, where the S2 teachers were using French to a considerable extent. But while their pupils made some effort to respond in French to teacher initiatives in that language, any spontaneous pupil initiative was always made in English.

Generally speaking the teachers at Sweet seemed to accept this state of affairs. They usually responded to pupils' L1-medium requests in French, but without insisting on reciprocity. Only one teacher was observed occasionally to reject L1 requests and to elicit FL phrases such as *Je voudrais une règle*. There was no systematic attempt on the Sweet teachers' part to anticipate likely pupil managerial initiatives and to teach appropriate FL exponents.

The situation was somewhat different at the two *Tour de France*-using schools, Palmer and Bloomfield. The *Tour de France* course includes in the language syllabus for active pupil mastery a range of exponents for common classroom requests, which all the teachers at these two schools were teaching, or had taught.

At Bloomfield High School, pupils in all classes were observed at times to make appropriate, spontaneous use of these previously taught managerial phrases:

TH	Work with your partner for a few minutes on that! *Vous allez travailler avec votre partenaire!*
P	*Je n'ai pas de partenaire!* (S1 class)
	....
TH	*Ecrivez la date*
P	*J'ai oublié mon crayon*
TH	*Qui va donner un crayon à X?* (S1 class)

They could not always be relied on to do so, however, and incidents in which the teacher insisted on their use occurred in most lessons:

TG	(Holding up flashcard) We are now in the Garnier family
P1	Miss, I can't see
TG	*Je n'ai pas compris!*
P1	(...)
TG	*Je n'ai pas compris!* What do you say if you can't see?
P2	*Je ne vois pas bien*
P1	*Je ne vois pas bien*
TG	*Voilà* (Holds card higher) *Oui? Bon, d'accord* (S1 class)

At Bloomfield, such incidents rejecting L1 initiatives by pupils, and insisting that French be used, happened only when the teacher felt an appropriate FL exponent had previously been taught. There was no general expectation that pupils would attempt to produce original messages in French.

Only at Palmer High School was there such a generalised expectation. A range of classroom management and discourse repair phrases were taught, and widely used by the pupils, especially in S2. Teachers did not usually react to re-use of these phrases (or variants of them) with any evaluative comment on their form. Instead, they gave a direct FL response to the pupil's message:

P   *Est-ce que je peux ouvrir la fenêtre?*
TB   *Bon, il y a une fenêtre ouverte, ça suffit. Alors tu ôtes ton anorak. Ote ton anorak!*

      ....

P   *Madame, je n'ai pas de crayon!*
TB   *Qui a un crayon, pour ce garçon misérable qui n'a pas de crayon?*

Where pupils attempted to produce original messages, the teachers' reaction was usually the same, even if the pupil utterances were imperfectly realised:

(Teacher B has been explaining procedure for a listening test)

P   *Toi parler?*
TB   *Oui, moi je vais parler, il n'y a pas de bande* (S2 class)

Where Palmer pupils failed to use French for managerial purposes, the teachers frequently insisted that they do so, supplying appropriate language material if necessary:

P   (referring to an activity sheet) Do we do the other side?
TC   *Comment est-ce qu'on dit ça en français?*
P   *Emm... page deux?*
TC   *Oui* (S2 class)

      ...

TC   *Encore cinq phrases, dans vos cahiers, comme ça, hein? Commencez! Oui?*
P   *(...) dans la salle de...* art
TC   *Comment? Tu n'as pas de crayon, ou quoi? Hein?*
P   Miss, it's in art. I left it there
TC   *Ton crayon, oui? Au dessin, oui? Dans la salle de dessin?*

P	*Oui*
TC	*Zut! Alors répète. J'ai laissé mon crayon -*
P	*J'ai laissé mon crayon -*
TC	*Dans la salle de dessin*
P	*Dans la salle de dessin*
TC	*Tu es bête, toi*
P	*Tu es bête, toi*

(General laughter) (S2 class)

While the use of English for managerial purposes was not completely barred even at S2 level, Palmer S2 pupils were usually expected to ask permission before using it:

P	*Madame*
TB	*(...)*
P	*Est-ce que je peux explique en anglais un moment?*
TB	(to a different pupil) *Ne mets pas ta veste comme ça, s'il te plaît. Attention au fil! Voilà*
P	*Est-ce que je peux explique en anglais un moment?*
TB	*Qu'est-ce que tu veux expliquer en anglais?*
P	*Ehh... Est-ce que je peux parler anglais un moment, s'il vous plait?*
TB	*Oh. C'est important?*
P	*Oui*
TB	*Tu ne peux pas le dire en français?*
P	*Non*
TB	*Vas-y!*
P	Madame, is ehh water pistols allowed in school?
TB	*Non!*
P	I've just been squirted by one!
TB	*Non, on ne doit pas avoir de... de pistolets d'eau dans le... au collège. Alors, alors, non!* (S2 class)

At S1 level, however, just as the teachers themselves used English more frequently without any special comment, L1 use by pupils for any extensive managerial exchanges was tolerated.

CONCLUSION

The Stage 2 observation at the different schools indicated that extensive FL use for classroom management purposes was feasible, given a higher level of personal commitment (and FL fluency) on the part of individual teachers, and also an ability to sustain a positive working atmosphere; a concerted departmental approach seemed helpful even to the most committed individual teachers. Some managerial moves did seem easier for teachers to make in French than others; several who were unwilling to commit themselves to exclusive FL use were happy to use French at least for the more routine, organisational moves, while FL use for 'activity instructions' was the preserve of the most committed teachers only, given its requirement for a flexible repertoire of communication and repair strategies.

Special efforts seemed to be required if pupils were to reciprocate their teachers' managerial use of French on any regular basis. The explicit teaching of an appropriate repertoire of exponents, plus persistent rejection of pupils L1 initiatives, seem to be necessary to bring this about. In the absence of active pressure of this kind from the teacher, it appears that pupils will not spontaneously adopt the FL as their own language of self-expression in the FL classroom, even where the teachers have done so to a considerable extent.

CHAPTER 8

CONCLUSION

To anyone concerned with bringing about changes and innovation in the context of the British foreign language classroom, the picture presented in the foregoing pages of this report must bring much encouragement. The patterns of teaching observed in the classrooms of these 'committed' teachers show significant differences when compared with those seen in our earlier study (Mitchell et al 1981). While oral practice FL activities predominated in both groups of classrooms, the rigid structure-drilling observed in 1977-78 had considerably softened in CI project classrooms, with the virtual disappearance of repetition drills and the contextualisation of many structural exercises. The regular reference being made by the teachers to behavioural objectives, the at least partial organisation of syllabus material on functional rather than structural principles, and the routine use of non-whole-class, cooperative organisational patterns (notably pair work), were new features in the later lessons. The communicative use of the target language had been considerably extended, both through its increased use for classroom management purposes, and through a greater frequency of teaching/learning activities involving the message-orientated, creative use of French (most notably, of open ended role play).

Of course, an explanation for these differences might be sought merely in the fact that different, smallish-sized groups of teachers were involved in the two research studies (and more especially in the fact that the teachers in the first study were a randomly selected group, whereas in the later study efforts were made to locate teachers with a commitment to 'communicative' teaching). While this explanation may account for some of the differences between the practices of the two groups, it seems that the two studies may genuinely reflect a shift occurring more generally in the ranks of the FL teaching profession. In support of this claim, firstly, the testimony of the CI project teachers themselves may be advanced. It emerges from the interview data reported in Chapter 1 that the teachers involved with this research perceived themselves as currently undertaking a fundamental reshaping of their own objectives and methodology, involving a move away from an essentially structuralist approach similar to that documented in the earlier study. Secondly, even during the course of the CI project itself, this change could actually be observed to a limited extent. Some teachers were seen in the course of adapting their own teaching strategy, with some individuals significantly increasing the communicative use of French in their classrooms between the observational and action research stages of the project.

This evidence of methodological development among teachers was perhaps one of the most important things to come out of this research study. It demonstrates that what must be a critical factor for foreign language learning, the quality of the classroom language environment, is alterable, on the initiative of the individual teacher (or group of teachers). Even in the British context, there are, apparently, no insuperable cultural constraints preventing the teacher who is motivated to do so from providing an almost completely FL-medium environment - provided he or she promotes an appropriate range of teaching/learning activities, and has also personally mastered (or transferred from L1) a key set of FL simplification and communication strategies to facilitate communicative FL use. This project also provided an opportunity to document and analyse the strategies actually used for this purpose by a group of skilled FL-using teachers, which hopefully can serve as a model for others interested in creating a similar quality of classroom language experience.

The project thus also re-emphasises the critical importance of the teacher as the central classroom resource, in any communicative teaching strategy. While up-to-date textbooks and certain 'authentic' materials (audiorecordings, pen pal letters, etc) were in use in the CI project classrooms, teacher-pupil interaction (mostly teacher-led) created the bulk of the FL linguistic environment for these learners, for very natural reasons. No functional syllabus, 'authentic' materials, or microcomputer programme can replace the capacity of the live, fluent speaker to hit upon the follow-up topics of interest to particular individuals, continually adjust his/her speech to an appropriate level of difficulty and solve unpredictable communication difficulties from moment to moment, or to 'scaffold' the learner's attempts at FL speech. In all this, the teacher and his/her interactive skills are decisive.

As well as documenting certain significant changes in the quality of classroom language experience, and the critical role of the teacher in initiating and sustaining these, the project also demonstrated the existence of considerable elements of continuity both in teachers' beliefs about language learning, and in their classroom practices. Even teachers strongly committed to providing extensive classroom experience of message-orientated FL use appeared to believe that at certain stages in the teaching/learning process both the analytic study of the structure of the target language and systematic practice in its forms had positive contributions to make. In the majority of CI project classrooms, the commonest teaching/learning activities involved FL practice (though often this meant rehearsal of functional exponents rather than of grammatical structures *per se*). Communicative activities, while more frequent than in the earlier study, tended to fall at the end of a fairly traditional sequence, from presentation to practice to use, and in some classrooms, the bulk of communicative FL experience was provided through the use of French for managerial and organisational purposes, rather than through any significant use of open-ended FL-medium teaching/learning activities. Altogether, few teachers appeared to have accepted that unconscious acquisition through exposure to naturalistic language use might be the only, or even the most significant, language development process operating in the FL classroom. Communicative FL use was a desirable enrichment of classroom experience, but for most teachers was not its core element.

The resulting pragmatic mixture of communicative and practice FL use, of linguistic analysis and exposure to unanalysed language performance, of course concealed certain tensions. One major unresolved issue concerned the type of syllabus that might most appropriately underlie a communicative approach to FL teaching. Most teachers in the CI project were following textbooks whose syllabuses were organised on partly functional, partly structural principles. This compromise appeared operable at this elementary stage. In particular, the functional organisation (and labelling) of language material had certain advantages: it seemed to make sense to the pupils, and facilitated the contextualisation of practice language activities as well as providing coherent blocks of language material quickly usable in role play and personal conversation. But some teachers appeared concerned lest in the longer term, such a pattern of syllabus organisation might hinder the learner's development of a creative FL system. There was, however, no consensus over the extent to which structural principles for syllabus organisation should be used at different stages, nor indeed over whether, and when, the conscious study of grammar (very rare in the S1 and S2 lessons observed for the CI project) should be introduced.

The S1/S2 lessons observed also concentrated strikingly on using and developing oral, interactive FL skills. This may be perfectly appropriate in the elementary stages of FL learning (after all, it mirrors the route of L1 acquisition). But clearly, in the longer term, a 'communicative approach' to FL teaching must also attend to the development of learners' extended receptive skills (reading and listening), as well as to writing. The CI project provides little evidence on possible 'communicative' approaches to these areas of FL competence.

It has been suggested above that the teachers sustained a pattern of L1 and practice FL use alongside communicative FL use, partly because of their beliefs about their possible contribution to FL learning. Another possible reason also emerged from the project, however: it appears that certain 'costs' may be involved in maximising communicative target language use in the classroom. In particular, it seemed from certain of the action research studies, that a commitment to operate through French alone was a constraint on the type of content that might be communicated about. Whether 'for real' in the small talk of classroom life, or in role play settings, everyone (teacher and pupils alike) seemed most comfortable with communicative uses of the target language which were primarily phatic and instrumental. When information content grew dense or reached any significant level of abstraction (as must be the case, for instance, in explaining a grammar point), most teachers either turned to English or cut the topic short; the few who soldiered on in French were likely to run into such density of comprehension difficulty as to find the maintenance of student attention difficult. And the quality of pupil contributions to classroom discussions was always severely restricted, if a requirement that they speak French exclusively was sustained. Again, of course, the teacher usually found a pragmatic, compromise solution; but overall, it seemed that at least some of the intellectual challenge which might in general be expected of secondary schooling must be sacrificed, if pupils are to build up extensive experience of confident and fluent FL use, both as listeners and as speakers, at least in the elementary stages.

Most of the teachers in this study nonetheless had few doubts about the value of the stronger emphasis they were attempting to place on FL communication in the classroom. As we have seen, they found their focal role as the initiator and sustainer of FL medium talk stressful and tiring; given this experience, group support from fellow staff members was critical in sustaining high levels of FL use. But clearly most teachers were deriving considerable job satisfaction from the new sense of purpose supplied by the goal of communicative competence, and by the new patterns of working.

And what of the pupils? No miracles were happening, in terms of levels of linguistic attainment being achieved; it is clear that the acquisition of language through informal exposure is a long term business, and dramatic results cannot be expected from the provision of a certain increase in communicative FL experience over the time perspective of S1/S2. But it was the teachers' overall impression that levels of motivation and involvement were being better sustained among their pupils. Most strikingly, by comparison with the lessons observed in 1977-78, the CI project lessons provided learners with rich opportunities to develop and try out a range of communication strategies, receptive and productive, so as to exploit to the full the limited language resource at their disposal; and the data quoted throughout this report show the confident extent to which these were availed of. The approach to elementary FL teaching documented in these pages appears to make sense to pupils: to provide them with objectives which they understand and with a varied range of enjoyable activities for which they see some point, and to build their confidence enough to 'have a go' in speaking the target FL. Whatever direction the 'communicative approach' may take at more advanced stages, this seems a healthy foundation upon which to build.

BACKGROUND LITERATURE

COMMUNICATIVE COMPETENCE

Theories of communicative competence enlarge traditional views of what it is to know a language to embrace not only knowledge of a linguistic system (phonology, grammar and vocabulary), but other knowledge and skills which enable that linguistic system to be put to use in real life interaction. Hymes' original (1971) formulation of the notion of communicative competence has been followed by others (see review by Canale and Swain, 1980). For example, a recent framework proposed by Canale for application in L2 pedagogy has four main components:

1. Grammatical competence (including phonology, orthography, vocabulary, work formation, sentence formation)

2. Sociolinguistic competence (expression and understanding of social meanings appropriate to different sociolinguistic contexts, and of grammatical forms appropriate to their expression)

3. Discourse competence (knowledge of different linguistic genres, together with their related devices for cohesion and coherence)

4. Strategic competence (ways of coping with grammatical, sociolinguistic, discourse and performance difficulties) (Canale, 1983)

Foreign language teaching in Britain, as elsewhere, has traditionally concentrated on the first of Canale's four elements, grammatical competence. The first central challenge of the 'communicative' movement to language teaching is therefore the enlargement of instructional activity to help learners also to master the other, traditionally somewhat neglected, dimensions.

LANGUAGE ACQUISITION

Students of first language acquisition have become increasingly convinced of the centrality of interpersonal communication in the young child's development of language (see various articles in Snow and Ferguson, eds, 1977). In a recent review article, Wells concludes that it is

> ... *from frequently repeated experiences of combining linguistic and nonlinguistic strategies in communicating about objects and events that come within the field of intersubjective attention, (that) the child gradually masters the linguistic system and its relation to the interpersonal and ideational meanings it serves to encode.* (Wells, 1981, p 108)

Others have argued that even in classroom settings, the mechanisms of L2 acquisition are likely to parallel those of L1 acquisition fairly closely (McLaughlin, 1978), and therefore that the context provided for L2 learning in the classroom should be as like as possible to that of L1 acquisition (Macnamara, 1975). Developing this perspective, Krashen (1981, 1982) argues that the most significant requirement of the L2 learner is a flow of 'comprehensible input' in the target language, i.e. message-orientated experience of the language, controlled for comprehensibility rather than for structure, and without any pressure on the learner to produce comparable, formally correct FL 'output'. He argues that the classroom teacher is well placed to provide this experience for L2 learners in the early stages, who are not yet ready to cope directly with real life communicative experience. Others writing recently in this area have, however, viewed the role assigned to the learner by Krashen's 'input' hypothesis as too restricted, and re-stressed the significance for learning of active and productive involvement in L2 interaction (e.g. Long, 1981, 1983; Allwright, 1984a, 1984b).

Foreign language teaching in Britain has traditionally given a great deal of attention to the conscious, analytic study of linguistic systems: to knowing about the target language. The second major theory-based challenge presented by the 'communicative' movement to L2 teaching is thus the question of how best to mimic in the classroom the linguistic and interactional context within which L1 is (almost universally) successfully acquired.

CURRICULUM DEVELOPMENT INITIATIVES IN SCOTLAND

The *Tour de France* Project

In 1975 the Scottish Central Committee on Modern Languages (SCCML) set up a working party convened by Richard Johnstone of Stirling University to produce materials for teaching French to children of all 'ability levels' in S1/S2 (Johnstone, 1980). In the event this project ran until 1984, by which time it had produced a complete French course, in five stages, for the 12-16 age range (i.e. covering the years S1-S4). The S1/S2 materials were piloted and evaluated in 1979-81 (Parkinson et al, 1982); the final package being published by Heinemann includes assessment materials (diagnostic and summative), and a wealth of methodological suggestions (in the form of 'Teachers' Books' accompanying each 'Stage'), as well as a range of teaching materials including Pupils' Books, and Workbooks, audiotapes, filmstrips and flashcards (SCCML 1982a, 1982b, 1983, 1984). After the pilot phase, which involved c. 40 schools in 1979-81, the course has been widely adopted and is currently the most commonly used in Scotland in S1/S2.

The Strathclyde *Eclair* initiative

In the later 1970s the Modern Languages Advisers of Strathclyde Region became interested in the *Eclair* French course being produced by the Inner London Education Authority (ILEA) and published by Mary Glasgow, again for secondary school beginners (ILEA, 1975). At first recommended to schools as material suitable for the 'less able', especially in S2, the course was soon made the basis for a more widely conceived curriculum development initiative. Led by divisional advisers, local working groups of teachers were established, to develop ancillary material to support the use of *Eclair* with all S1/S2 pupils. These groups produced syllabus documents identifying functional objectives for various units of *Eclair*, assessment materials (in the form of profile sheets), and methodological recommendations in the form of Teachers' Notes; the extensive documentation produced in this way was circulated to schools and made the basis for in-service activity in the region. By 1980 *Eclair* was in use in the majority of Strathclyde schools at S1/S2 level.

The Lothian *Graded Levels of Achievement in Modern Languages* (GLAFLL) project.

This project was started in 1976, on the initiative of Lothian Region's Assistant Adviser in Modern Languages (Clark, 1980). It undertook as its first task the development of functional/notional syllabuses for the full range of languages taught in Lothian schools, akin to the Council of Europe's *Threshold Level* syllabuses, but aimed at school age beginners. Syllabus development (again the work of teachers' groups, with advisorate support) was rapidly followed by the production of schemes of graded tests, on the basis of which regional certificates of achievement were awarded.

Teachers involved in the GLAFLL project were encouraged to be self-reliant as far as materials were concerned, either adapting existing coursebooks or producing their own within the school. However, while GLAFLL never concerned itself with materials production, by 1980 the attention of the project leaders had shifted to methodology, and this became a major focus of documentation, including video materials production, and of in-service activity. GLAFLL produced a long series of documents in mimeo form (e.g. Clark and Hamilton, n.d.); the syllabuses plus some other material have also been published by CILT (Clark and Hamilton, 1984a, 1984b and 1984c).

These Scottish initiatives paralleled a much larger number of developments in England, where the Graded Objectives in Modern Languages (GOML) movement linked dozens of curriculum and assessment development projects in different local authority areas. The Council of Europe's 1971-1981 Modern Languages Project provided important theoretical insights for all these British projects especially in the area of curriculum design, mainly through its promotion of functional notional syllabus models (e.g. Van Ek, 1975; Coste et al, 1976); additionally, the Project provided a framework for contacts with theoretical and practical developments in other countries. Overall, the 'communicative approach' is now sufficiently broadly based in British schools and sufficiently mature for its influence to be apparent in various projects for the reform of national and regional public examination systems.

COMMUNICATIVE METHODOLOGY

Classroom process issues were given relatively little attention in the early stages of the British movement for the renewal of FL teaching, by comparison with issues of syllabus, materials development and assessment. (A group from the Council of Europe Modern Languages Project, visiting schemes in Britain in 1980, remarked on this: Bergentoft, 1983. Their view is echoed in the overview of the GOML movement produced by key figures within it: Harding, Page and Rowell, 1980.) However, more attention was subsequently paid to methodological principles (e.g. by Clark, 1981; Hawkins, 1981; Littlewood, 1981 and Dunning, 1982.) A new generation of coursebooks and teaching materials (predominantly for the teaching of French) is rich in practical methodological suggestions; courses such as *Tricolore* (Honnor, Hold and Mascie-Taylor, 1980; Honnor and Mascie-Taylor, 1981), *Action* (Buckby, 1980, 1981 and 1982) and *Salut* (ITE, 1983 and 1984), as well as *Tour de France* and *Eclair*, share a commitment to developing the learner's communicative competence, and make methodological proposals accordingly.

THE INTERVIEW SCHEDULE AND CONDUCT OF THE INTERVIEWS

The interview schedule developed for use in this phase of the project's work is reproduced as Figure A2.1

As can be seen, apart from the collection of some basic data on the extent and duration of teachers' involvement in innovation, the interview was not concerned with the specifics of individual curriculum projects. Instead, the intention was to elicit teachers' general understandings of the concept of 'communicative competence', their views about its place among the objectives of common course language teaching, and the implications of consciously adopting such an objective for syllabus and methodology. Teachers were to be encouraged to refer to their own practical experience as much as possible, to express doubt and criticisms, and to talk about problems and constraints.

The interview schedule was meant to function as a guide for the interviewer, rather than being administered in a rigidly structured manner. Thus, for example, the order in which topics were discussed was to some extent responsive to the concerns of the interviewees, who often raised particular issues ahead of the related question being asked of them by the interviewer.

The 59 teachers were interviewed individually, with interviews generally lasting between 40-60 minutes. With the teachers' permission, all interviews were audiorecorded, and the recordings were subsequently transcribed.

Figure A.2

Teacher interview schedule, Stage 1

(Permission to record)

(Confidentiality)

1. How long have you been involved with Project X?

2. What classes are you using Project X with?
   - S1/S2 or above?
   - mixed ability/sets?

3. What was the process of introducing Project X like?
   - Departmental meetings?
   - Outside advice?

4. Are you involved in activity outside the school involving Project X?
   - Regional/national WPs?
   - Talks at in-service meetings?

5. Why did your department get involved with Project X?
   - Motivations to innovate?
   - Attractions of Project X?
   - Any other reasons?

6. What for you are the **new** things in Project X, compared with what you were doing before?

7. Moving away from Project X for the moment - as you know, I am interested in the current concern with 'communication' in FL teaching. Firstly, the idea of 'communicative FL competence', as a goal for FL teaching - could you outline your current understanding of this?

   (CLARIFY-   a) in relation to Project X,
                     b) in relation to FLT in general).

8. Are you in sympathy with the idea of 'communicative FL competence' as a major objective in FLT?

9. How does 'communicative competence' as an objective fit in with the general purpose(s) of FLT in schools?
   - a major/minor role?
   - any conflicts with other possible goals?
   - any qualifications depending on pupil ability level?

10. What are the implications of a commitment to 'communicative competence' as an objective, for
    - syllabus? (incl. progression)
    - assessment?
    - methodology?

11. Within the area of methodology, what would a communicative approach be like?
    What are its implications for
    - what gets talked about
    - activities
    - class organisation
    - classroom management
    - attitudes to error
    - T/P relations
    - teaching grammar
    - teaching writing?

12. What innovations (compared with current practice) would be required in these areas to adopt a fully 'communicative' approach? How much of this happens already?

13. What are the problems and constraints likely to be met with in adopting a communicative approach?
    - teachers' own FL competence?
    - resource and time constraints?
    - class size/management?
    - assessment constraints?

14. What is the proper **balance** to be aimed at between **communicative** and **practice** FL activities?

15. What has your own experience been like in trying to implement a 'communicative' methodology?
    - successes?
    - constraints?

16.}

17.} (Not administered)

18.}

19. Next year, we shall be conducting a further phase of this project, working intensively with a small number of departments to try and investigate in the classroom the problems and possibilities of adopting a fully communicative approach.

    Would you be interested in involving yourself in this further stage?

    (*Expressions of interest at this stage do not involve a commitment!*)

20. Anything you would like to add or to ask me?

THE OBSERVATIONAL VISITS

The first round of Stage 2 visits all took place during the first term of the 1981-82 school year. On this occasion each participating teacher was observed throughout the fortnight, working with one or two classes at first or second year level. A total of 122 lessons was observed during these visits, or an average of almost nine lessons per teacher. (The lessons varied in timetabled length from 40 minutes to 65 minutes; total timetabled time for French also varied across schools, from 185 to 240 minutes per week). Details of the lessons seen are given in Table A3.1.

Table A3.1

French lessons observed, Autumn 1981

School	French course in use in S1/S2	No. of teachers participating	Lessons observed
Palmer H S	*T de F*	4 (Teachers A,B,C,D)	19 S1 19 S2 (40 mins ea.)
Bloomfield H S	*T de F*	4 (Teachers E,F,G,H)	12 S1 16 S2 (1 hr + ea.)
Sweet G S	*Eclair*	3 (Teachers I,J,K)	8 S1 21 S2 (40 mins ea.)
Jespersen Academy	*Tricolore*	2 (Teachers L,M)	8 S1 19 S2 (40 mins ea.)

Extensive notes were taken on each lesson seen during these visits, and a proportion was audiorecorded. The teachers were interviewed at some length concerning the observed pattern of teaching, but at this stage the researcher made no 'interventionist' proposals. The activities seen thus constituted the teachers' interpretation of a 'communicative' approach to FL teaching (though of course guided to a greater or lesser degree by the development project in which they were involved, and the materials they were using). While trying to go on teaching as usual, the teachers were of course aware of the purposes of the research visits and may have been influenced, consciously or unconsciously, to make extra efforts with these classes.

This was not seen as a disadvantage, as the research design assumed a positive commitment to a 'communicative approach' among participating teachers.

'Interventionist' visits

The second round of Stage 2 visits, to the same four modern language departments, were mostly made during the third term of the 1981-82 school year, though one school (Jespersen) was not re-visited until the first term of the 1982-83 year. A total of twelve teachers was included in the second round of visits.

The researcher again followed these teachers' work with one or two S1 or S2 French classes. Indeed, most of the classes were the same as those seen on the first occasion. However, the research strategy adopted for this visit was different. Instead of generalised observation, specific types of teaching activity identified on the first round of visits as being of particular interest in the quest to promote communicative FL use were made the object of small scale, 'interventionist' studies. One or two such studies were jointly planned by the researcher and each participating teacher, and completed within the fortnight's visit. The key lessons in which the activities under investigation were tried out by the teachers (sometimes with more than one class) were recorded for later study, a range of pupil attitudinal and performance data was collected, and preliminary evaluations were made in discussion between the teacher concerned and the researcher.

BIBLIOGRAPHY

Alderson, J C and Hughes, A H (eds) (1981) *Issues in Language Testing*. ELT Documents no. 111. London: The British Council.

Allwright, R L (1984a) 'The importance of interaction in classroom language learning'. *Applied Linguistics* 5,2: 156-171.

Allwright, R L (1984b) 'Why don't learners learn what teachers teach? The interaction hypothesis' In Singleton, D M and Little, D G (eds) (1984): 3-18.

Bergentoft, R (1983) *Project No 4 'Modern Languages' (School Sector): Consolidated Report on the Network*. Strasbourg: Council of Europe.

Brumfit, C J (ed) (1983) *Learning and Teaching Languages for Communication: Applied Linguistic Perspectives*. London: CILT

Brumfit, C J (ed) (1986) *The Practice of Communicative Teaching*. English Language Teaching Documents no. 124. Oxford: Pergamon.

Buckby, M (1980) *Action! Book 1*. Sunbury on Thames: Nelson.

Buckby, M (1981) *Action! Book 2*. Sunbury on Thames: Nelson.

Buckby, M (1982) *Action! Book 3*. Sunbury on Thames: Nelson.

Canale, M (1983) 'From communicative competence to communicative language pedagogy'. In Richards, J C and Schmidt, R W (eds) (1983): 2-28.

Canale, M and Swain, M (1980) 'Theoretical bases of communicative approaches to second language teaching and testing.' *Journals of Applied Linguistics* 1,1: 1-47.

Clark, J L (1980) 'Lothian Region's project on Graded Levels of Achievement in Foreign Language Learning'. *Modern Languages in Scotland* 19: 61-74.

Clark, J L (1981) 'Communication in the classroom'. *Modern Languages in Scotland* 21/22: 144-156.

Clark, J L and Hamilton, J (n.d.) *Syllabus Guidelines for a Graded Communicative Approach Towards School Foreign Language Learning. Part 1: Communication.* Edinburgh: Lothian Regional Council.

Clarke, M and Handscombe, J (eds) (1983) *On Tesol 1982: Perspectives on Language Learning and Teaching.* Washington DC: TESOL.

Coste, D, Courtillon, J, Ferenczi, V, Martins-Baltar, M, Papo, E and Roulet E (1976) *Un Niveau-Seuil.* Strasbourg: Council of Europe.

Dunning, R (1982) 'Communicative methods at 16+'. In Lunt, H (ed) (1982): 21-29.

Faerch, C and Kasper, G (1980) 'Processes and strategies in FL learning and communication'. *Interlanguage Studies Bulletin (Utrecht)* 5,1: 47-118.

Faerch, C and Kasper, G (eds) (1983) *Strategies in Interlanguage Communication.* Harlow: Longman.

Gump, P V (1967) *The Classroom Behaviour Setting: Its Nature and Relation to Student Behaviour.* Final Report, Project no. 2453, US Department of Health, Education and Welfare.

Harding, A, Page, B and Rowell, S (1980) *Graded Objectives in Modern Languages.* London: CILT.

Hatch, E (1979) 'Interaction, input and communication strategies'. Paper presented at the First Nordic Symposium on Interlanguage, Helsinki.

Hawkins, E (1981) *Modern Languages in the Curriculum.* Cambridge: Cambridge University Press.

Honnor, S, Holt, R and Mascie-Taylor, H (1980) *Tricolore 1*. Leeds: E J Arnold.

Honnor, S and Mascie-Taylor, H (1981) *Tricolore 2*. Leeds: E J Arnold.

Hymes, D H (1971) 'On communicative competence'. In Pride, J B and Holmes, J (eds) (1972): 269-293.

Inner London Education Authority (1975) *Eclair: A Three Year Multimedia Course in French*. London: Mary Glasgow Publications.

Institiuid Teangeolaíochta Éireann (1983) *Salut Book 1*. Dublin: Educational Company of Ireland.

Institiuid Teangeolaíochta Éireann (1984) *Salut Book 2*. Dublin: Educational Company of Ireland.

Johnstone, R (1980) 'An interim outline of the *Tour de France* syllabus for first-year classes' *Modern Languages in Scotland* 19: 34-50.

Johnstone, R (forthcoming) *A Handbook of Communicative Methodology*. Department of Education, University of Stirling.

Krashen, S D (1981) *Second Language Acquisition and Second Language Learning*. Oxford: Pergamon.

Krashen, S D (1982) *Principles and Practice in Second Language Acquisition*. Oxford: Pergamon.

Littlewood, W T (1977) 'Defining communication in foreign language teaching'. *Linguistische Berichte* 52: 83-92.

Littlewood, W T (1981) *Communicative Language Teaching: An Introduction*. Cambridge: Cambridge University Press.

Long, M H (1981) 'Input, interaction and second language acquisition'. In Winitz, H (ed) 1981: 259-278.

Long, M H (1983) 'Native speaker/non-native speaker conversation in the second language classroom'. In Clarke, M and Handscombe, J (eds) (1983): 207-225.

Lunt, H (ed) (1982) *Communication Skills in Modern Languages at School and in Higher Education.* London: CILT.

McLaughlin, B (1978) *Second-Language Acquisition in Childhood.* Hillsdale, N J: Lawrence Earlbaum Associates.

Macnamara, J (1975) 'Comparison between first and second language learning'. *Working Papers in Bilingualism* 12.

Mitchell, R (1982) 'The foreign language teacher as communicator: some Scottish evidence'. *Journal of the Irish Association for Curriculum Development* 11, 2: 33-41.

Mitchell, R (1983a) 'The teacher's use of first language and foreign language as means of communication in the FL classroom'. In Brumfit, C J (ed) (1983): 41-58.

Mitchell, R (1983b) 'Coping with communication'. *Modern Languages in Scotland* 24: 76-86.

Mitchell, R (1985) 'The use of role play tasks in assessing FL communicative performance'. *British Journal of Language Teaching* 23, 3: 169-172.

Mitchell, R and Johnstone, R (1981) *Communication in the Foreign Language Part 1: Introduction.* Foreign Language Teaching Materials Package 1. Department of Education, University of Stirling.

Mitchell, R and Johnstone, R (1986) 'The routinisation of communicative methodology'. In Brumfit, C J (ed) (1986): 123-143.

Mitchell, R, Parkinson, B and Johnstone, R (1981) *The Foreign Language Classroom: An Observational Study.* Stirling Educational Monographs no. 9. Department of Education, University of Stirling.

Morrow, K (1981) 'Communicative language testing: revolution or evolution'. In Alderson, J C and Hughes, A H (eds) (1981): 9-25.

Parkinson, B, McIntyre, D, and Mitchell, R (1982) *An Independent Evaluation of* 'Tour de France'. Stirling Educational

Monographs no. 11. Department of Education, University of Stirling.

Pride, J B and Holmes, J (eds) (1972) *Sociolinguistics*. Harmondsworth: Penguin.

Richards, J C and Schmidt, R W (eds) (1983) *Language and Communication*. Harlow: Longman.

Scottish Central Committee on Modern Languages (1982a) *Tour de France* 1. London: Heinemann Educational Books.

Scottish Central Committee on Modern Languages (1982b) *Tour de France* 2. London: Heinemann Educational Books.

Scottish Central Committee on Modern Languages (1983) *Tour de France* 3. London: Heinemann Educational Books.

Scottish Central Committee on Modern Languages (1984) *Tour de France* 4. London: Heinemann Educational Books.

Sinclair, J McH and Brazil, D (1982) *Teacher Talk*. Oxford: Oxford University Press.

Sinclair, J McH and Coulthard, M (1975) *Towards an Analysis of Discourse*. Oxford: Oxford University Press.

Singleton, D M and Little, D G (eds) (1984) *Language Learning in Formal and Informal Contexts*. Dublin: Irish Association for Applied Linguistics.

Snow, C E and Ferguson, C A (eds) (1977) *Talking to Children*. Cambridge: Cambridge University Press.

Tarone, E (1980) 'Communication strategies, foreigner talk, and repair in interlanguage'. *Language Learning* 30, 2: 417-431.

Van Ek, J A (1975) *The Threshold Level*. Strasbourg: Council of Europe.

Wells, G (1981) *Learning Through Interaction*. Cambridge: Cambridge University Press.

Winitz, H (ed) (1982) *Native Language and Foreign Language Acquisition*. Annals of the New York Academy of Sciences 379.

KEY TO ABBREVIATIONS

CFL — Communicative Foreign Language

CI project — Communicative Interaction project

EFL — English as a Foreign Language

FL — Foreign Language

FLT — Foreign Language Teaching

GLAFLL — Graded Levels of Achievement in Foreign Language Learning

GOML — Graded Objectives in Modern Languages

L1 — First language, i.e. mother tongue

L2 — Second - foreign - language

PFL — Practice Foreign Language

S1-4 — Years 1 to 4 of secondary schooling (Scotland)

SCCML — Scottish Central Committee on Modern Languages

SEB — Scottish Examinations Board

Printed in the United States
By Bookmasters